A Students
AutoSketch

A. Yarwood

Longman
Scientific &
Technical

Longman Scientific & Technical,
Longman Group UK Limited,
Longman House, Burnt Mill, Harlow,
Essex CM20 2JE, England
and Associated Companies throughout the world.

Copublished in the United States with
John Wiley & Sons, Inc., 605 Third Avenue, New York, NY 10158

First published 1992

British Library Cataloguing in Publication Data
Yarwood, A.
  A students AutoSketch.
  I. Title
  604.20285

  ISBN 0–582–08383–4

Library of Congress Cataloging-in-Publication Data
is available for this title

Set in Melior (Linotron 202)
Produced by Longman Singapore Publishers (Pte) Ltd.
Printed in Singapore

A Students AutoSketch

Contents

List of Plates (between pages 116 and 117)

Preface

AutoSketch is an inexpensive CAD (Computer Aided Drawing) software package. Despite its low cost, complicated 2D (two-dimensional) drawings can be speedily and accurately constructed with its aid.

In educational establishments AutoSketch is being used for two purposes:
1. as a general introductory program for learning how to construct drawings with the aid of CAD software;
2. as a general introduction to AutoCAD.

AutoCAD has become the world's most used CAD software package and is installed as the drawing software of choice in many colleges of Further and Higher Education with departments or faculties of engineering, building or architecture. To become proficient in drawing with AutoCAD requires time and practice. AutoSketch is reasonably easy to use and after learning how to draw with its aid, acquiring proficiency in constructing drawings with AutoCAD becomes much easier.

This book contains details of how to draw with both the MS–DOS and the Archimedes version of the software. Because an Archimedes version 3 is not available, details of drawing with the MS–DOS version 3 of the software are given (page 152) and for drawing with the Archimedes version 2. However, most but not quite all of the methods given here also apply to versions 1 and 2 of the software.

Some of the methods of drawing described in the pages of this book are my own adaptations for using the software to various constructional methods. Examples are: the methods of section hatching; the construction of pictorial drawings; drawing isometric ellipses and using them as Part files. The reader may find interest in developing his/her own construction methods in a similar manner. AutoSketch is a CAD system that lends itself to such developments.

All the drawing illustrations in the book were drawn with the aid of AutoSketch version 2 software, some worked on an IBM compatible PC and some on an Archimedes 310. All drawings were plotted to a Roland DXY-880A plotter, many being drawn with two, sometimes three, thicknesses of pens fitted to the plotter.

The contents of the book form a course of work for those wishing to familiarise themselves with and become expert with using this software. The graded series of exercises in its pages will assist the reader to achieve these aims.

A disc containing starter drawing files for all seventy-two drawing exercises in the book is available (details on page 151). If this disc is purchased, readers wishing to learn the use of AutoSketch will be able to work the exercises much more quickly. This is because when each starter for an exercise is loaded to the computer screen from this disc, much of the preliminary construction work will have been completed. This will allow the reader to practise the work for which the exercise has been designed, without having to go through the preliminary constructions on which the exercise is based.

Salisbury 1991   A. Yarwood

Acknowledgements

We are indebted to the following for permission to reproduce copyright material:

British Standards Institution for symbols from BS 3939 and BS 308. Complete copies of the documents can be obtained from BSI at Linford Wood, Milton Keynes, MK14 6LE.

Registered trademarks

CHAPTER 1

Introduction

AutoSketch is an inexpensive computer-aided drawing (CAD) software package, providing a good two-dimensional (2D) drawing system. With its aid, technical drawings and technical illustrations can be quickly and accurately drawn: engineering and architectural drawings for various disciplines; technical graphics such as charts, diagrams, posters and the like.

The contents of this book are based on the assumption that the reader has access to a computer with equipment suitable for working with AutoSketch version 2. The software can be either the AutoSketch package designed for an IBM compatible PC (personal computer) or that for an Archimedes computer.

The AutoSketch manual describes how the software is installed and the computer configured for running the software. The computer and equipment setup requirements are:

1. The computer must have at least 512 kbyte of RAM.
2. Although drawing can be carried out with only the cursor keys, some form of pointing device to control the positioning of the pointer on screen is desirable. This can be one of:
   (a) a mouse;
   (b) a trackerball;
   (c) a joystick.
3. AutoSketch can be run on an IBM PC without a math coprocessor, but if one is fitted, the speed of drawing is increased ten-fold. If the computer is an Archimedes, a Floating Point Emulator (as a ROM module) is supplied with the software. This ensures a fast drawing speed.
4. The equipment should include a printer or plotter to print or plot drawings on to paper (hardcopy).

AutoSketch can be run either from a floppy-disc drive or from a hard disc. If working with AutoSketch version 1 most but not all of the methods of drawing described in this book can be employed.

Starting up AutoSketch

When AutoSketch has been installed to the instructions given in the software's manual, start-up depends upon the type of equipment in use – whether working from a floppy-disc drive or a hard-disc drive, with an IBM compatible PC or with an Archimedes computer. In the following descriptions:

Keyboard – the letters, figures or words are to be typed in at the computer keyboard;

Return – the Return (or Enter) key of the computer is to be pressed.

If working with AutoSketch installed on the hard disc, with the AutoSketch directories and files in the directory C:\SKETCH, on an IBM compatible PC the following brings AutoSketch into action:

C:\> cd sketch
C:\SKETCH> sketch *Keyboard Return*

OR

C:\> CD SKETCH *Keyboard Return*
C:\SKETCH> SKETCH *Keyboard Return*

When working with AutoSketch in a floppy disc drive – say drive A:, start-up requires typing the following at the A: prompt:
A:\> floppy *Keyboard Return*
A:\> sketch *Keyboard Return*

AutoSketch can be started up direct from the C:\> prompt if a batch file SKETCH.BAT is saved to the hard disc. This file can be made and saved by typing in the following sequence:
C:\> copy con sketch.bat *Keyboard Return*
cd sketch *Keyboard Return*
sketch   *Keyboard Return*
cd..   *Keyboard Return*
^Z   *Keyboard Return (save file sketch.bat)*
      1 File(s) copied

and the file SKETCH.BAT will be saved on the hard disc. Note ^Z = press Ctrl key and key Z.

Then to start-up AutoSketch from the hard disc all that is required is:
C:\> sketch *Keyboard Return*

If working with an Archimedes, the computer itself will normally start up in Drive 4 if a hard disc is fitted and in Drive 0 if a hard disc is not fitted. If a hard disc is fitted and AutoSketch is to be run from Drive 0, the software is started up by typing:

*drive 0   *Keyboard Return (switches from drive 4 to drive 0)*
*fpe   *Keyboard Return* (to initiate floating point emulator)
*sketch   *Keyboard Return*

OR

*FPE
*SKETCH *Keyboard Return*

If AutoSketch is already on the hard disc, all that will be needed is to type:

*fpe   *Keyboard Return*   or   *FPE Keyboard Return*
*sketch   *Keyboard Return*   or   *SKETCH Keyboard Return*

The AutoSketch drawing screen

AutoSketch works through:

1. *pull-down menus*, each with a series of
2. *menu items* (commands), some of which are set by
3. *dialogue boxes* which appear centrally on screen;
4. the positioning of the AutoSketch *arrow pointer* under the control of the pointing device (or the cursor keys if no pointing device is available).

All the menus, menu items and dialogue boxes will be discussed and illustrated in this book.

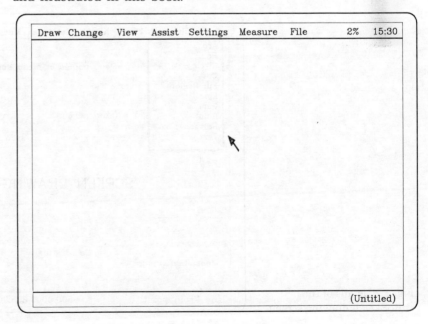

Fig. 1.1 The AutoSketch drawing screen

When AutoSketch is first started up the monitor screen appears as in Fig. 1.1 (The AutoSketch drawing screen).

Figure 1.2 shows the various parts of the AutoSketch drawing screen. These are:

1. Menu bar – the names of the pull-down menus always show at the top of the screen on the *menu bar*. In Fig. 1.2 the **Draw** menu has been pulled down displaying its menu items.

2. Memory used – with IBM compatible PC machines, the drawing memory available for construction is displayed as a percentage figure on the menu bar. With Archimedes machines this is displayed in the form of the kilobytes of memory available.

3. Time – is constantly being up-dated on the menu bar in digital form. The accuracy of the time is of course dependent upon the computer's clock being correct.

4. Screen drawing area – most of the screen is available for constructing drawings.

5. The AutoSketch Arrow pointer – its position is controlled by the pointing device for positioning points, for constructing drawings, for selection of menus and menu items, for pointing at items within dialogue boxes.

6. Prompt line – the following may appear on the prompt line:
    (a) on the left – when a menu item (command) has been

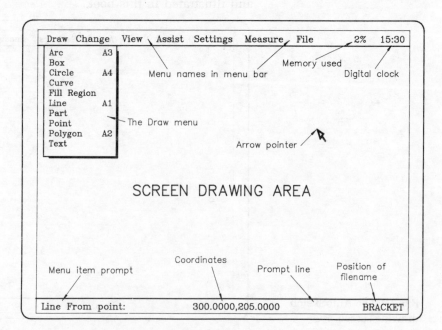

Fig. 1.2 Details of the AutoSketch drawing screen

selected, its name with prompts telling the operator what action to take;

(b) in the centre, if the menu item Coords is On – the x,y coordinate position of the arrow pointer;

(c) on the right – the title of the file name of the drawing being constructed.

7. Note that the style of text used for menu names, menu items and lettering in dialogue boxes for the MS–DOS AutoSketch screen is different from that used in the Archimedes AutoSketch screen.

8. Some of the spellings of details in AutoSketch are American – the software was originated in the USA.

Function key selection of menu items

Twenty of the menu items can be selected without the pull-down menus, by pressing one of the function keys or by pressing a combination of an Alt key and a function key. If the computer being used is an Archimedes, either the Ctrl or the Shift key is used in place of the Alt key for this purpose.

The twenty keys or combinations of keys are:

Function key F1	– Undo	(Alt+F1) A1	– Line
F2	– Redo	A2	– Polygon
F3	– Erase	A3	– Arc
F4	– Break	A4	– Circle
F5	– Move	A5	– Ortho on/off
F6	– Copy	A6	– Grid on/off
F7	– Stretch	A7	– Snap on/off
F8	– Pan	A8	– Attach on/off
F9	– Last view	A9	– Group
F10	– Zoom box	A10	– Ungroup

Or – in the case of an Archimedes machine

Function key F1	– Undo	(Ctrl or Shift+F1) C1	– Line
F2	– Redo	C2	– Polygon
F3	– Erase	C3	– Arc
F4	– Break	C4	– Circle
F5	– Move	C5	– Ortho on/off
F6	– Copy	C6	– Grid on/off
F7	– Stretch	C7	– Snap on/off
F8	– Pan	C8	– Attach on/off
F9	– Last view	C9	– Group
F10	– Zoom box	C10	– Ungroup

If these twenty menu items are called by taking advantage of the F and Alt+F (or Ctrl+F) keys, the rate at which drawings can be constructed with AutoSketch will be faster than if menu items are always selected from menus. This is because it is often much quicker to press, e.g., F10 to **Zoom box**, than to first point at the **View** menu and when that appears to point at **Zoom box**. After some experience with drawing with AutoSketch, the key calls will be memorised. To assist the memory for the calls, a strip of paper or card such as is shown in Fig. 1.3 can be sellotaped to the top of the keyboard. Some keyboards have a special holder for such F key calls.

The operator will soon learn when it is quicker to use a key call for a menu item or select from a menu. A combination of both methods will be found to produce the fastest results.

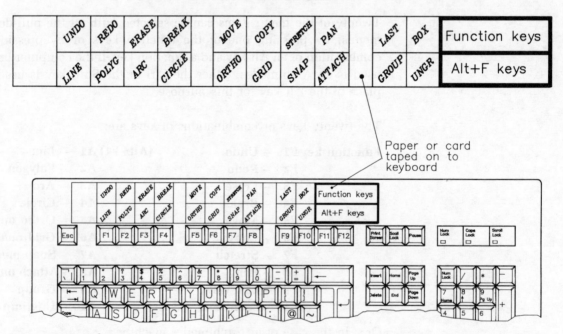

Fig. 1.3 A paper or card
function key reminder

Highlighting

When a menu name, a menu item or an item in a dialogue box is pointed at by the AutoSketch arrow pointer, its name or the box for the item is highlighted – i.e. the name or the box in which the name, letters or figures appear, changes colour. Figure 1.4 indicates the highlighting of the word **Draw** when the menu name is pointed at by the AutoSketch arrow. The highlighting indicates that:

1. When a menu name is highlighted and the button of the pointing device pressed, its menu is pulled down.
2. When a menu item is highlighted and the button of the pointing device pressed, a prompt associated with the item appears on the prompt line and the command becomes active.
3. If a menu or a menu item is pointed at by mistake, pointing at the correct, required item automatically cancels that selected in error.
4. If a mistake is made when using a menu item, selecting the item again from its menu will automatically cancel out the mistake and the correct operation for the item can then be made.
5. In dialogue boxes when a name, a number or **OK** is pointed at and the button of the pointing device pressed, the name or number is accepted as being correct.

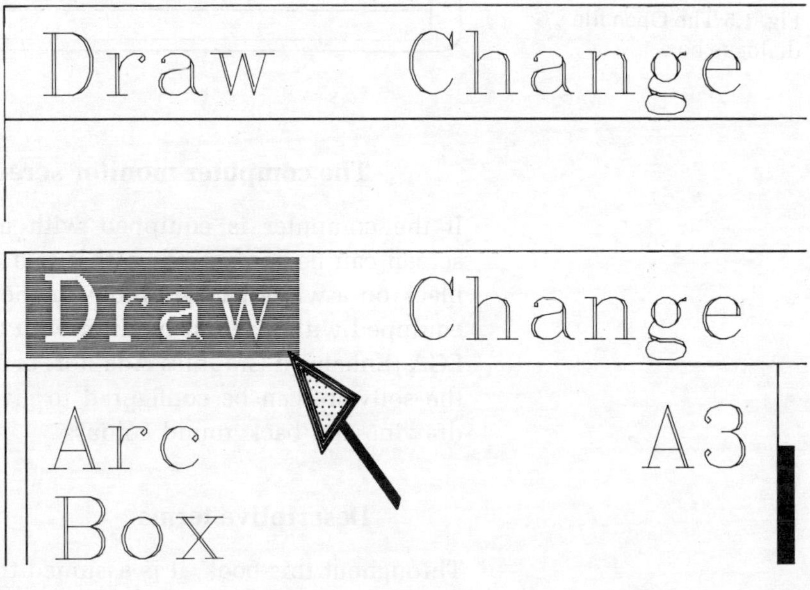

Fig. 1.4 The menu word
Draw highlighted

Figure 1.5 shows one of the many dialogue boxes which appear in the centre of the screen when some menu items are selected. That shown is when the menu **File** has been selected and the menu item **Open** then chosen from the resulting pull-down menu.

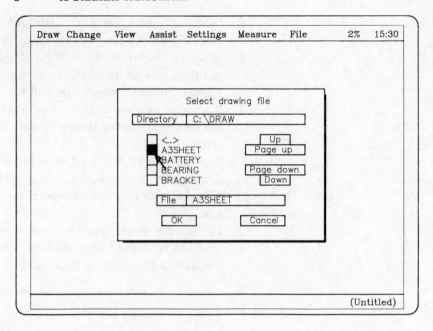

| Draw | Change | View | Assist | Settings | Measure | File | 2% | 15:30 |

Select drawing file

Directory C:\DRAW

<..>
A3SHEET
BATTERY
BEARING
BRACKET

Up
Page up

Page down
Down

File A3SHEET

OK   Cancel

(Untitled)

Fig. 1.5 The Open file
dialogue box

The computer monitor screen

If the computer is equipped with a monochrome monitor, the
screen can be configured so that text and drawing lines appear in
black on a white background – or the inverse – white on black. If
equipped with a colour monitor with the appropriate colour card –
EGA (Enhanced Graphics Adaptor) or VGA (Video Graphics Array),
the software can be configured to give one from a choice of four
drawing and background colours.

Descriptive terms

Throughout this book, it is assumed that a pointing device such as
a mouse is in use. This is for positioning and dragging the
AutoSketch pointer arrow around the drawing area of the screen.
To pull down a menu, activate a menu item or set an item in a
dialogue box when it has been highlighted, the button of the
pointing device must be pressed. Although a pointing device is
assumed, the descriptions could equally as well apply if only the
cursor and Return (Entry) keys are available. The descriptions of
methods of working throughout the book follow a pattern such as:

Menu	Item	Action
1. **Settings**	**Limits**	Dialogue box settings:

	Right	420	*Keyboard*	*OK*
	Top	297	*Keyboard*	*OK*

Some follow the pattern:

Prompt	Action
1. **Line From point:**	100,200 *Keyboard button*
2. **Line To point:**	R(120,0) *Keyboard button*

In these examples, the terms involved have the following meanings:

Menu — select the menu name from the menu bar and press the button of the pointing device;

Item — select the named item from the named menu and press the pointing device button;

Prompt — detail of the prompt(s) as they appear at the prompt line;

Action — the action to be taken;

Keyboard — the preceding word, letters and/or figures are to be typed in at the prompt line from the computer keyboard;

Button — press the button of the pointing device;

Return — press the Return (or Enter) key of the computer keyboard;

OK — point at the letter OK in the dialogue box and press either the Return key or the button of the pointing device;

Point — point at the menu, menu item or detail with the AutoSketch arrow under the control of the pointing device and then press the button of the device.

Note: when the description of a method of working applies to a dialogue box, it is assumed that the **OK** of the dialogue box will be pointed at and the pointer device button pressed to accept the stated settings.

Exercises

The following exercises are questions requiring short answers, some only one word. They are included here to allow the reader quickly to revise the various topics introduced in the chapter.

1. Can three-dimensional drawing be constructed in AutoSketch?
2. What is meant by the terms: pull-down menu; command;

pointing device; menu item.

3. Can AutoSketch be used for drawing without a pointing device being fitted to the computer?

4. What is the advantage of fitting a math coprocessor to a PC when using AutoSketch?

5. How is AutoSketch brought into action: from the hard disc of a PC? from a floppy disc of a PC? from the hard disc of an Archimedes? from a floppy disc of an Archimedes?

6. What is the purpose of the file SKETCH.BAT?

7. Name the parts of the AutoSketch drawing screen.

8. What menu items can be brought into action by pressing the function keys 1 to 10?

9. What is meant by the term highlighting?

10. What are the minimum memory requirements for a computer on which AutoSketch can be run?

CHAPTER 2

Construction of drawing outlines

The Draw pull-down menu

Select **Draw** from the menu bar, i.e., move the AutoSketch pointer arrow to the word Draw and press the mouse button (click). The **Draw** menu appears – Fig. 2.1. Except for two items, the commands in this menu are for the construction of elements (objects) of the outlines of drawings. The exceptions are **Fill Region** and **Part**. **Part** will be fully described later in Chapter 6.

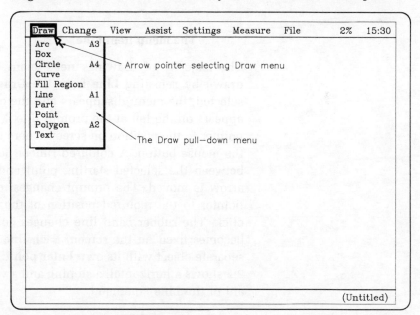

Fig. 2.1 The Draw pull-down menu

Before going any further, practise drawing any outlines with the aid of each of the drawing commands in the **Draw** menu. Don't bother yet to try producing meaningful drawings, just practise with each command in turn to get the feel of how they function in producing outlines on screen.

Some examples are given in Figs 2.2 to 2.4.

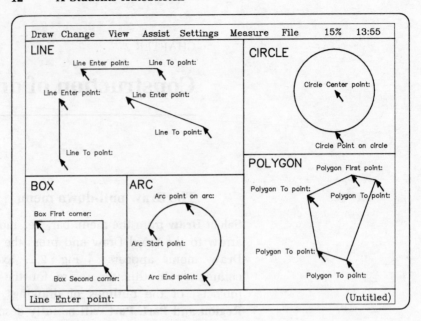

Fig. 2.2 Drawing with the Line, Circle, Box, Arc and Polygon menu items

The menu item Line

The majority of drawings need many straight lines. These are drawn by selecting **Line** from the **Draw** *pull-down* menu. When selected, the menu disappears and the command **Line Enter point:** appears on the left at the prompt line. Move the AutoSketch arrow pointer to the position on screen where the line is to start and click the mouse button. A coloured *rubber band* line now appears from between the selected starting point and the pointer arrow as the arrow is moved. The prompt changes to **Line To point:** Move the pointer to the required position of the other end of the line and click. The rubber band line changes colour and the required line becomes fixed on the screen. Each line drawn in AutoSketch is a separate object with its own **Enter point:** and **To point:** ends. Figure 2.2 shows a horizontal, a sloping and a vertical line drawn with the aid of the **Line** command.

The menu item Circle

When **Circle** is selected from the Draw menu, the prompt **Circle Center point:** appears at the prompt line. After selecting the required centre with the pointer arrow, the prompt changes to **Circle Point on circle:**. Select the required point and the circle appears on screen.

The menu item Box

Select **Box** from the **Draw** menu, the menu disappears and **Box First corner:** appears at the prompt line. When this First corner has been selected the prompt changes to **Box Second corner:** When the second corner has been selected the required rectangle appears on screen. Any size rectangle can be drawn with this menu item by selecting its diagonally opposite corners. Figure 2.2 gives an example of a box.

The menu item Arc

When **Arc** is selected from the **Draw** menu **Arc Start point:** appears at the prompt line. After selecting the start point, a second prompt **Arc Point on arc:** appears. When this second point has been selected, a final prompt **Arc End point:** requests selection of the end of the arc, which then appears on screen.

The menu item Polygon

To AutoSketch a polygon is a straight-sided, open or closed figure with as many sides as the operator wishes. The first prompt **Polygon First point:** is followed by repeated **Polygon To point:** prompts. The ends of lines of AutoSketch polygons are joined to each other. When, either the mouse is double clicked, or when the polygon **First point** is pointed at a second time, the outline of the polygon become fixed on screen. The double clicking anywhere during the construction of a polygon allows an open straight-line figure to be drawn. Clicking on the **First point** after drawing the required polygon closes the outline of the figure. Figure 2.2 shows the drawing of a closed polygon.

The menu item Curve

Curves are drawn within a framework of straight lines. The frame can either be seen as the curve is constructed or not seen as desired. If the frame is to be seen, point to **Assist** on the menu line. The resulting pull-down menu includes an item **Frame** as shown in Fig. 2.13 on page 19. Pointing at the word causes a tick to appear against the item. When so selected the **Curve** frame surrounding the curved outline appears – Fig. 2.3. Note that when drawing a curve the joins of the curve frame are selected by pointing – not by pointing on the curve itself. It will be seen later (pages 44–5) that

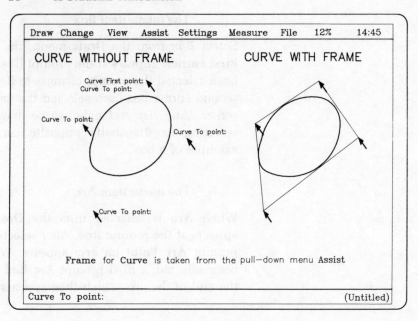

Fig. 2.3 Drawing with the
Curve menu item

the shape of a curve can be changed with the aid of the **Stretch** command from the **Change** pull-down menu.

The menu item Fill Region

To create a solid-filled region, select this command and proceed as if drawing a closed Polygon, selecting the corners of the area to be filled one after the other. Upon selecting the **Fill Enter point:** start point a second time, the area enclosed is automatically solid filled. (Fig. 2.4.)

The menu item Text

Before selecting this command from the **Dra**w menu, the text font and its size should be set. Select **Settings** from the menu bar. The pull-down menu which results includes the item **Text**. Select this item and the dialogue box Fig. 2.5 appears.

With the aid of the pointing device, a selection can be made from several fonts, each of which can be given a height, an angle at which it is to be drawn, a width and an obliquing angle. This allow selection from a variety of fonts of different heights, angles, widths and slope. Figure 2.6 indicates some possible fonts for inclusion with drawings when **Text** is in operation. When **Text** is selected from the **Draw** menu, the prompt **Text Enter point:** appears. When

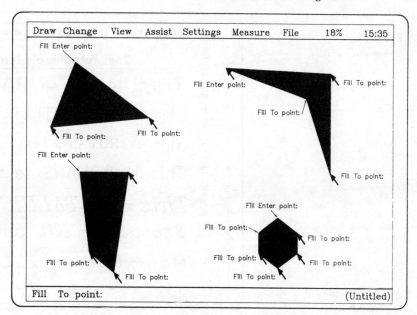

Fig. 2.4 Drawing with the Fill region menu item

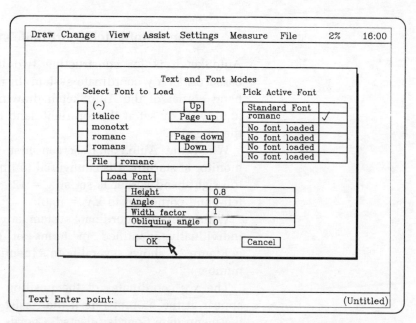

Fig. 2.5 The Text dialogue box

this has been selected, the prompt changes to **Text Enter text:** As the text is being typed at the command line, it appears at the prompt line and on screen. Pressing the mouse button will fix the text on screen and place the start point for the next line of text immediately below the start of the text already on the screen. Press the *Return* key and the **Text Enter point:** prompt re-appears at the prompt line.

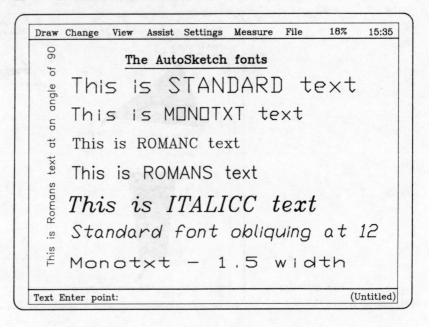

| Draw Change View Assist Settings Measure File   18%   15:35 |

The AutoSketch fonts

This is STANDARD text

This is MONOTXT text

This is ROMANC text

This is ROMANS text

This is ITALICC text

Standard font obliquing at 12

Monotxt - 1.5 width

This is Romans text at an angle of 90

Text Enter point: (Untitled)

Fig. 2.6 Examples of
AutoSketch fonts

The AutoSketch coordinate system

AutoSketch is for constructing two-dimensional (2D) drawings based on an x,y coordinate system. In this system the bottom left-hand corner of the AutoSketch drawing screen is usually x,y = (0,0) with x,y set at the top right-hand corner to *limits* decided by the operator.

When the AutoSketch screen first appears on the computer monitor at startup, it is configured to limits of x,y = (12,9), i.e., the top right-hand corner is set at x = 12 and y = 9, with the bottom left-hand corner set to x,y = (0,0).

Within this 2D coordinate system, any point on the screen can be individually identified in terms of the two numbers x and y. Figure 2.7 shows several points identified by their x,y coordinate numbers.

The x,y coordinates of the position of the pointer arrow will appear at the prompt line if the **Assist** menu is pulled down and the menu item **Coords** selected. **Coords** can be switched **On** or **Off** by pointing at the item in the **Assist** menu (see Fig. 2.13 on page 19). A tick against the item shows that it is **On**.

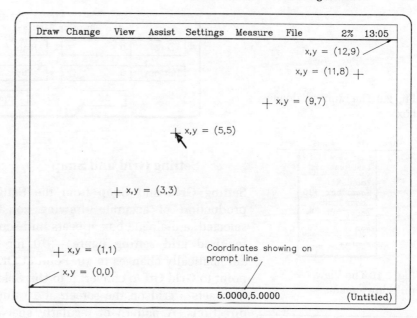

Fig. 2.7 Coordinate points on
the AutoSketch screen

Setting a screen to A3 limits

In order to construct drawings for metric A3 sheets, it is advisable
to set the screen limits to sizes suitable for drawing in metric
units. To do this it is necessary to set the screen limits to, e.g., x,y
= 420,297, which corresponds to A3 sheet sizes of 420 mm by
297 mm. Then each coordinate unit can be taken as representing
one millimetre drawn to a scale of 1:1. Other limits could be x,y =
297,210 (A4) or x,y = 594,420 (A2).

In order to set up a screen suitable for A3 (Figs 2.8, 2.9 and 2.10):

Fig. 2.8 The Settings pull-
down menu

Menu	Item	Action
1. **Settings**	**Limits**	Dialogue box settings:
		Right 420 *Keyboard OK*
		Top 297 *Keyboard OK*
		Dialogue box *OK*
2. **View**	**Zoom limits**	
3. **Settings**	**Grid**	Dialogue box settings:
		X Spacing 10 *Keyboard OK*
		Grid *point* **Off** changes to **On**
		Dialogue box *OK*
4. **Settings**	**Snap**	Dialogue box settings:
		X Spacing 5 *Keyboard OK*
		Snap *point Off* changes to **On**
		Dialogue box *OK*

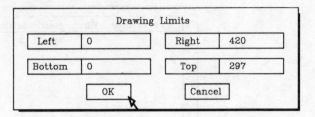

Fig. 2.9 The Limits dialogue box

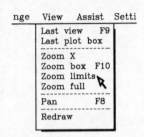

Fig. 2.10 The View pull-down menu

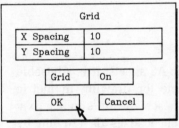

Fig. 2.11 The Grid dialogue box

Setting Grid and Snap

Setting **Grid** and **Snap** from the **Settings** menu assists in the production of accurate drawing constructions. When **Grid** is selected, a dialogue box appears mid-screen (Fig. 2.11). Typing the required grid setting figure – 10 for **X Spacing** – **Y Spacing** automatically changes to 10. Point at **OK** or press *Return* and then point to **Grid Off** to convert it to **On**. Selecting the dialogue box **OK** then sets a grid on the screen at 10 units in each of the *x* and *y* directions. A pattern of regularly spaced dots appears in screen (Fig. 2.12).

A similar dialogue box appears when **Snap** is selected from the **Settings** menu. When **Snap** is set and **On**, the pointer arrow locks onto the nearest snap position within the snap settings when it is moved. **Snap** and **Grid** can, if desired, be set independently to different spacings. They can also be set to independent spacings in the *x* and *y* directions.

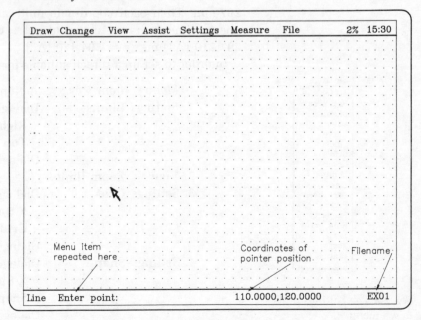

Fig. 2.12 A 10 units Grid in the AutoSketch screen

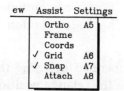

Fig. 2.13 The Assist pull-down menu

Switching Grid and Snap on and off

These two menu items can be switched on and off by pulling down the **Assist** menu (Fig. 2.13) and clicking onto Grid or Snap as required. If a tick is seen against either item, then that item is **On**. No tick means it is **Off**. Clicking onto the item switches it **Off** if **On** is showing and vice versa.

Absolute and relative coordinates

Accurate constructions can be obtained in *AutoSketch* with the aid of **Grid**, **Snap**, and the systems of *absolute* and *relative* coordinates. Figure 2.14 illustrates how a drawing composed of straight lines can be drawn to exact unit sizes based on x,y coordinates. This is an example of constructing to unit sizes with the aid of *absolute* coordinates. Absolute coordinate positions for the ends of the lines are given using the x,y coordinates of each line ending. The sequence of obtaining the correct outline in Fig. 2.14 followed the sequence on the prompt line:

Prompt	Action		
Line Enter point:	100,200	Keyboard	button
Line To point:	300,200	Keyboard	button
Line Enter point:	300,200	Keyboard	button
Line To point:	300,150	Keyboard	button

Fig. 2.14 Drawing lines to absolute coordinates

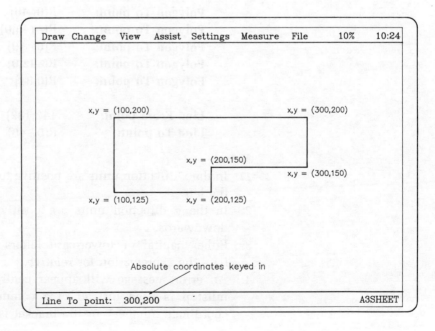

Line Enter point:	300,150	*Keyboard*	*button*
Line To point:	200,150	*Keyboard*	*button*

and so on around the whole outline.

Figure 2.15 is an example of an outline obtained by using the *relative* coordinate numbers system, in which the relative position of the **To point:** of each line is stated in relation to the **Enter point:** of the line.

The sequence in Fig. 2.15 follows the pattern:

Prompt	*Action*		
Line Enter point:	100,116	*Keyboard*	*button*
Line To point:	R(-42,0)	*Keyboard*	*button*
Line Enter point:	142,200	*Keyboard*	*button*
Line To point:	R(0,-84)	*Keyboard*	*button*
Line Enter point:	100,116	*Keyboard*	*button*
Line To point:	R(-42,0)	*Keyboard*	*button*

Another method would be to use **Polygon**. The following describes the sequence by which the whole straight line outline of Fig. 2.15 could be constructed:

Prompt	*Action*		
Polygon From point:	100,200	*Keyboard*	*button*
Polygon To point:	R(42,0)	*Keyboard*	*button*
Polygon To point:	R(0,-19)	*Keyboard*	*button*
Polygon To point:	R(143,0)	*Keyboard*	*button*
Polygon To point:	R(0,-46)	*Keyboard*	*button*
Polygon To point:	R(-143,0)	*Keyboard*	*button*
Polygon To point:	R(0,-19)	*Keyboard*	*button*
Polygon To point:	R(-42,0)	*Keyboard*	*button*
Polygon To point:	R(0,84)	*Keyboard*	*button*
		closes polygon	
Line From point:	142,182)	*Keyboard*	*button*
Line To point:	R(0,-46)	*Keyboard*	*button*

Notes

1. In the x direction units are positive to the right and negative to the left.
2. In the y direction units are positive upwards and negative downwards.
3. Either capital or lower-case letters can be used for the R (r) – the abbreviation for *relative*.
4. An error message will appear centrally on screen if, say, a fullstop is used instead of a comma between the x and y coordinate numbers, or if a bracket is missed.

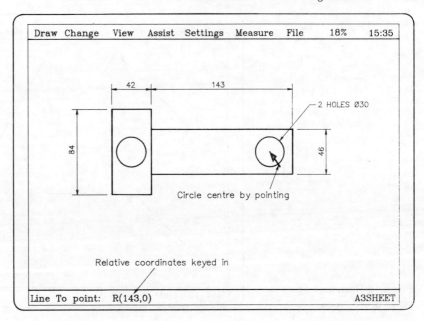

Fig. 2.15 Drawing lines to relative coordinates

The two circles of Fig. 2.15 could be drawn by either of the two methods:

Prompt	Action	
Circle Center:	121,158	*Keyboard button*
		x,y coordinates of centre
Circle Point on circle:	R(0,15)	*Keyboard button*
	or	
Circle Center:	*point*	*button at required centre*
Circle Point on circle:	R(0,15)	*Keyboard button*

Polar coordinates

Lines at angles to other lines can be accurately drawn with the aid of the Polar coordinate system. Figure 2.16 shows examples of the angles so drawn. After selecting the beginning of the angled line, either by pointing or by stating its absolute coordinate position, type in a P, followed by the length of the required line and its angle – followed by the length of line and its angle – (length of line, angle anti-clockwise from horizontal).

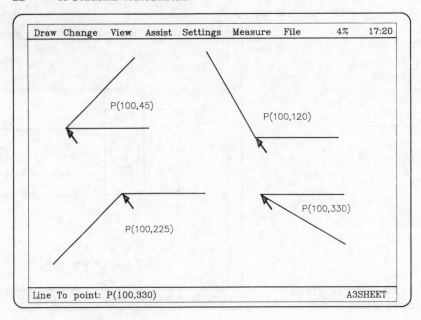

Fig. 2.16 Drawing angles to polar coordinates

Exercises

Each of the following exercises are designed to be drawn in an AutoSketch drawing screen set to **Limits** of x,y = 420,297 and with **Grid** set to 10 and **Snap** set to 5.

1. Draw, to any sizes, the four shapes given in Fig. 2.17. Use the menu items (commands) **Line** and **Circle** from the **Draw** menu.

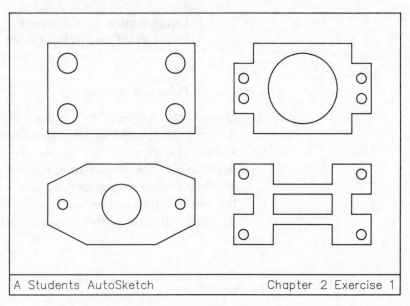

Fig. 2.17 Exercise 1

2. Draw to any sizes the outlines given in Fig. 2.18. Use commands **Line**, **Box**, **Arc** and **Circle** from the Draw menu.

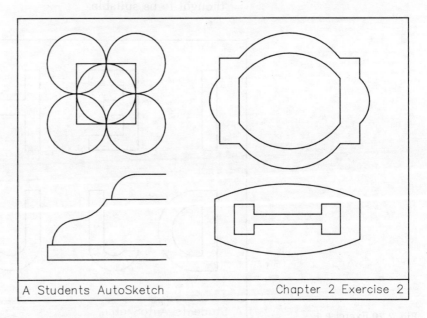

A Students AutoSketch   Chapter 2 Exercise 2

Fig. 2.18 Exercise 2

3. Using only the **Box** command from the **Draw** menu copy the drawing given in Fig. 2.19. Draw to any sizes thought to be suitable.

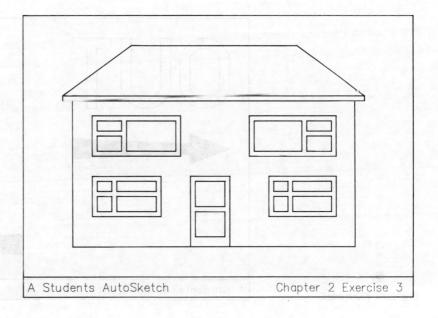

A Students AutoSketch   Chapter 2 Exercise 3

Fig. 2.19 Exercise 3

4. Draw the given letters shown in Fig. 2.20 using commands **Line**, **Polygon** and **Arc** from the **Draw** menu. Use any sizes thought to be suitable.

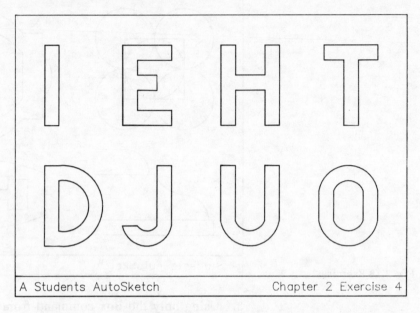

A Students AutoSketch   Chapter 2 Exercise 4

Fig. 2.20 Exercise 4

5. Using the commands **Line**, **Polygon**, **Arc** and **Fill Region**, construct the two signs shown in Fig. 2.21. Use any sizes thought to be suitable.

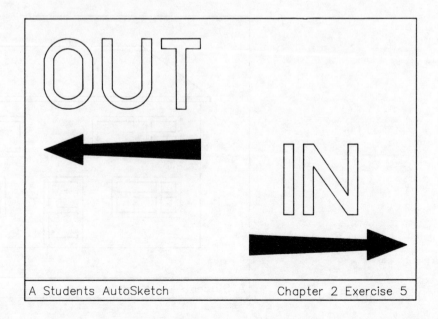

A Students AutoSketch   Chapter 2 Exercise 5

Fig. 2.21 Exercise 5

6. Construct the shapes shown in Fig. 2.22 with the aid of **Line** (Polar coordinates), or **Polygon**, together with **Arc** and **Text**. Draw to any suitable sizes.

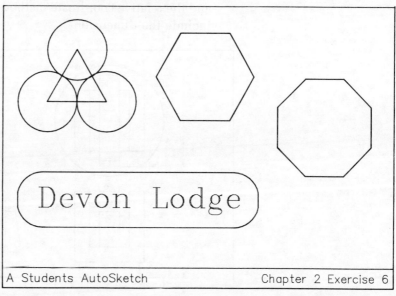

A Students AutoSketch — Chapter 2 Exercise 6

Fig. 2.22 Exercise 6

7. Copy the given three-view orthographic drawing shown in Fig. 2.23 using the commands **Circle, Line** and **Box** from the **Draw menu**. Work to the given dimensions with the aid of the **Grid** and **Snap** settings (10 and 5) together with the relative coordinates methods of determining lengths. Do not include the dimensions.

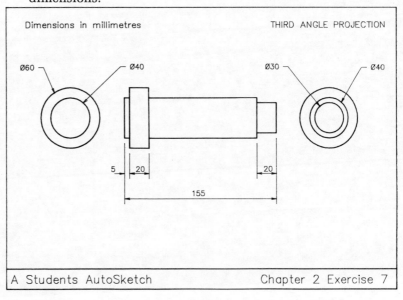

A Students AutoSketch — Chapter 2 Exercise 7

Fig. 2.23 Exercise 7

8. Copy the three-view orthographic projection given in Fig. 2.24 with the aid of commands **Line**, **Box**, **Circle** and **Text** from the **Draw** menu. Work to the sizes given with the aid of **Grid Snap** and the relative coordinate method of determining sizes. Do not include the dimensions.

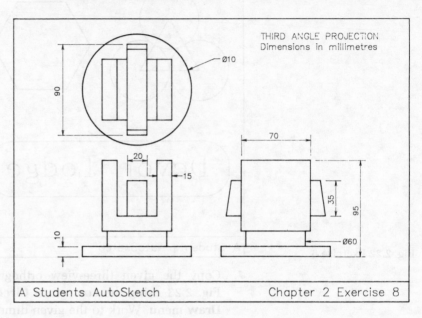

THIRD ANGLE PROJECTION
Dimensions in millimetres

Ø10

90

70

20

15

35

95

10

Ø60

A Students AutoSketch   Chapter 2 Exercise 8

Fig. 2.24 Exercise 8

CHAPTER 3

The Settings and Assist menus

The Settings menu

Reference has already been made to some of the menu items in the **Settings** menu. In Chapter 2 the **Settings** menu items **Limits**, **Grid**, **Snap** and **Text** were mentioned. In this Chapter the **Settings** menu items **Line type**, **Color**, **Units**, **Attach**, **Pick**, **Property** and **Curve** will be introduced. Other **Settings** menu items will appear in later Chapters as the need to set the items is required. Thus **Chamfer**, **Fillet**, **Box Array** and **Ring Array** will be introduced in Chapter 4 and **Part base** in Chapter 8. Figure 3.1 shows the items in the **Settings** menu.

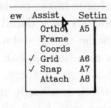
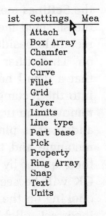

Fig. 3.1 The Settings and
Assist pull-down menus

The Assist menu

Figure 3.1 also shows the items in the **Assist** menu. A tick appearing against an item means that it is operative. To turn any one of these items on or off, point at the item and click – if a tick is present the item is turned off, if a tick is not against the item, it is turned on. Note that four of the items can also be switched on or off by pressing the Alt+function key 5 for **Ortho**; Alt+f6 for **Grid**; Alt+f7 for **Snap**; Alt+f8 for **Attach**. The menu items of the **Assist** menu have the following functions:

Ortho – switches on or off the drawing of lines orthogonally – when **Ortho** is on, lines can only be drawn vertically or horizontally.

Frame – switches on and off the frame lines surrounding curves when they are drawn. When Frame lines are included with a curve, its shape can be changed – see page 44.

Coords – if on the *x,y* coordinate positions of the pointer arrow are displayed at the prompt line.

Grid – turns grid dots on and off.

Snap – turns snap on and off.

Attach – if on, an object being drawn on screen will attach itself as near to an Attach point (End, Mid, Center or Node) as is determined by the setting of the pick interval.

Dialogue boxes

Each item in the **Settings** menu has its own *dialogue box*, which appears at the centre of the screen when the item is selected from the **Settings** menu. Dialogue boxes contain details of the settings for the selected menu item. To set a detail within a dialogue box, the rectangle beside the name of the detail is pointed at and clicked on. This either results in a tick appearing in the rectangle to show that a detail has been set, or in some, numbers have to be keyed into the rectangle. If a tick is already in a rectangle, clicking on it removes the tick, turning that detail off. When a number has to be added, it is placed in its appropriate rectangle by pointing at the rectangle and typing the necessary figure(s). A pair of rectangles then appear by the side of the selected detail in which **Cancel** and **OK** will be seen. If the number in the detail rectangle is correct, clicking on the **OK** sets the detail to that number. If the number is incorrect, clicking on the **Cancel** deletes it, ready for the correct figure(s) to be keyed into the rectangle. Finally, pointing at and clicking on the **OK** rectangle of the dialogue box sets all the details selected or keyed into the dialogue box and the dialogue box disappears from the screen. If all the settings in a dialogue box are already those which are required, click on the **Cancel** rectangle of the dialogue box and the dialogue box disappears from the screen.

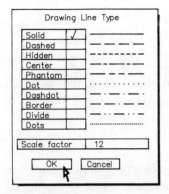

Fig. 3.2 The Line type
dialogue box

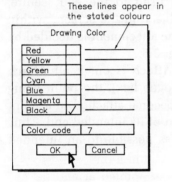

Fig. 3.3 The Colour dialogue
box

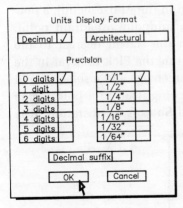

Fig. 3.4 The Units dialogue
box

The dialogue box Line type

AutoSketch can produce Arcs, Boxes, Circles, Curves and Lines in ten different Line types. These are shown in the **Drawing Line Type** dialogue box of Fig. 3.2. The default Line type is **Solid**, with a **Scale factor** of 0.5. This means that when AutoSketch is loaded into a computer it automatically produces Solid lines when drawing commands are in action. When working in metric for A sheet sizes, a different Scale factor must be keyed in. That shown – 12 – is suitable for drawing for A3 sheet size to a drawing scale of 1:1 (full size). When working to different scales and/or on different sheet size drawing, the Line type Scale factor will need to be changed to suit the sheet size and drawing scale.

The dialogue box Color

AutoSketch can draw in any one of seven colours. These are shown in the **Drawing Color** dialogue box of Fig. 3.3. Each colour is numbered from 1 to 7. These colour numbers are fairly standard throughout computing. For colours to show on screen, a colour monitor must be attached to the computer. On a mono monitor, the colours will show as different shades of grey.

The dialogue box Units

Selection of the required units, in the form of decimals or in the form of feet and inch units, is made within this box. See Fig. 3.4.

Various selections within this box produce dimensions displaying the formats:

Decimal	0 digits	300
Decimal	2 digits	35.00
Decimal	6 digits	73.000000
Decimal	3 digits	Decimal suffix mm 300.000mm
Architectural	1/4″	5 3/4″
Architectural	1/16″″	4′–10 9/16″

Note also that the **Limits** dialogue box changes in response to the Units selection. If Architectural units are selected the screen limits will be shown in the Drawing Limits dialogue box, for example:

| Left | 0″ | Right | 35′–0″ |
| Bottom | 0″ | Top | 25′–0″ |

For the same **Limits** settings, if Decimal units are selected, the

Drawing Limits dialogue box will show:

Left	0	**Right**	420
Bottom	0	**Top**	300

Note also that the Units selection also determines the units in which **Perimeter** is displayed within the **Area** dialogue box.

The dialogue box Attach

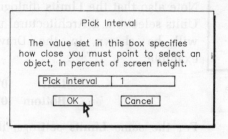

Fig. 3.5 The Attach dialogue box

In the **Attach** dialogue box of Fig. 3.5, all attachment modes are shown as being on. **Attach** will only operate if a tick is displayed against **Attach** in the **Assist** menu, showing that **Attach** is on. When **Attach** is on, when, e.g., a point is selected for the beginning of a line, that end of the line will attach itself to the end, centre, midpoint, etc., nearest to the chosen object on the screen, within the **Pick** interval area. The nearness of the attachment is decided by the setting within the **Pick** box. See Fig. 3.6.

Note: care must be exercised when **Attach** is on. If all **Attach** modes are in action (ticked in the dialogue box), the point being chosen – e.g., the end of a line – may become attached to a point such as the centre of another line instead of its intended end. Thus even with **Attach** on, pointing as near as possible to an intended **Attach** point is necessary.

The dialogue box Pick

Attach is associated with the **Pick** Interval shown in the **Pick** dialogue box (Fig. 3.6). **Attach** is important for achieving accurate drawings. When **Attach** is on (i.e. ticked in the **Assist** menu), a new line (say) will attach itself to the end, midpoint, quadrant point, centre or node point of the object on the screen nearest to the pointer arrow. Care is needed when setting the **Pick** Interval in the **Pick** Interval dialogue box. Too big a percentage and a selected end of line position (say) may end up attaching itself to a point some distance from where it was intended. If **Snap** is in operation, it is

Fig. 3.6 The Pick dialogue box

often not necessary to have **Attach** on from the **Assist** menu. The default setting of the **Pick Interval** of 1 (1% of screen height) is usually adequate for most drawing construction.

The dialogue box Property

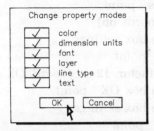

Fig. 3.7 The Properties dialogue box

In Fig. 3.7 this dialogue box is shown with all properties of objects which can be changed by the **Change** menu item **Property** (page 44). When the need to change the property of an object in a drawing does not include one or more of those shown as on in the **Property** dialogue box, then those not needed must be turned off by pointing at and clicking on those not needed in the change. As an example, if the Property Layer is ticked and the operator wishes to change a property, but not its layer, then the item Layer must be turned off by pointing at its tick in the dialogue box.

The dialogue box Curve

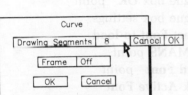

Fig. 3.8 The Curve dialogue box

The number of segments contained in a curve as it is being drawn is decided by the number keyed into this dialogue box. A large number of segments will slow down the speed with which the curve generates on screen, but will produce a more finely drawn curve; the default value of 8 can usually be accepted. (Fig. 3.8.)

Setting up an A3 sheet file

In order to work the exercises in Chapter 2, the reader was advised to set **Limits** to (420,297), set **Grid** to 10 and **Snap** to 5. These were set by selecting the menu items **Limits**, **Grid** and **Snap**, in turn from the **Settings** menu and completing the resulting dialogue boxes appearing central to the screen. A complete A3 drawing file, which can be opened before any work is attempted, can be set up as follows:

Menu	Item	Action
1. **Settings**	**Limits**	Dialogue box settings:
		Right 420 *Keyboard* *OK*
		Top 297 *Keyboard* *OK*
		Dialogue box **OK** *point*
2. **Settings**	**Grid**	Dialogue box settings:
		X Spacing 10 *Keyboard* *OK*
		Grid *point* to **Off**
		(changes to **on**)
		Dialogue box **OK** *point*

3. **Settings   Snap**   Dialogue box settings:
                           X Spacing 5 *Keyboard   OK*
                           Dialogue box **OK**   *point*

4. **Assist   Coords**   Dialogue box settings:
                           Coords   *point*
                           (turns Coords **on**)

5. **Settings   Line type** Dialogue box settings:
                           Solid   *point*
                           Scale factor 12 *Keyboard   OK*
                           Dialogue box **OK**   *point*

6. **Settings   Color**   Dialogue box settings:
                           Black   *point*
                           Dialogue box **OK**   *point*

7. **Settings   Units**   Dialogue box settings:
                           Decimal   *point*
                           0 digits   *point*
                           Dialogue box **OK**   *point*

8. **Settings   Text**   Dialogue box settings:
                           Select Font to load
                           ROMANS *point*
                           Load Font   *point*
                           Pick Active Font
                           ROMANS *point*
                           Height 6 *Keyboard   OK*
                           Dialogue box **OK**   *point*

9. **View   Zoom limits**
   drawing screen zooms to limits, showing up the 10
   units grid pattern of dots.

10. **File   Save as** Dialogue box settings:
                           File name A3sheet *Keyboard*
                           OK
                           Dialogue box **OK**   *point*

and a drawing file A3SHEET.SKD will be saved to disc.
When a new drawing is to be started:

Menu	*Item*	*Action*
File	**Open**	Dialogue box settings
		File name A3SHEET *point OK*
		Dialogue box **OK** *point*

and the prepared A3 sheet drawing appears on the AutoSketch
drawing screen, which will then be set up for drawing as if on an

```
A3 sheet drawing file

Menu:   Settings

Menu item:   Limits:      420,297

Menu item:   Grid:        10   On

Menu item:   Snap:         5   On

Menu item:   Coords:      On

Menu item:   Line type:   Solid   (default)

Menu item:   Color:       Black   (default)

Menu item:   Units:       Decimal   0 digits

Menu item:   Text:        Romans   Height 6

Menu:   File

Menu item:   Save as:     a3sheet

    File saved with filename a3sheet.skd
```

```
Other default settings

Menu item:   Attach:   Off
Menu item:   Chamfer:  0.5
Menu item:   Curve:    8
Menu item:   Fillet:   0.5
Menu item:   Pick:     1
Menu item:   Property: All on
```

Fig. 3.9 Details of an A3
sheet drawing file

A3 size drawing paper. In this drawing and working to a scale of 1:1, each coordinate unit will represent 1 millimetre. See Fig. 3.9:

Using A3SHEET.SKD and the Settings menu items

Figure 3.10 is an example of a simple engineering drawing constructed in AutoSketch. The procedures for constructing it were as follows:

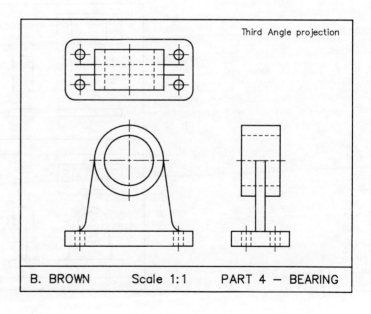

Fig. 3.10 An orthographic
drawing in an A3 sheet

Menu	Item	Action
1. **File**	**Open**	Dialogue box settings: **Select drawing file A3SHEET** point Dialogue box **OK** point
2. **Draw**	**Polygon**	Draw outlines (drawing 1 of Fig. 3.11)
3. **Draw**	**Circle**	Draw circles (drawing 2 of Fig. 3.11)
4. **Draw**	**Line**	Draw lines (drawing 3 of Fig. 3.11)
5. **Change**	**Break**	Break lines in end view (drawing 3 of Fig. 3.11)
6. **Settings**	**Fillet**	Dialogue box settings: **Fillet radius** 10 Keyboard OK Dialogue box **OK** point

Note that the menu item **Fillet** is described in Chapter 4 (page 51)

7. **Change**	**Fillet**	Add fillets (drawing 4 of Fig. 3.11)

Note: some lines will have to be renewed as fillets are drawn

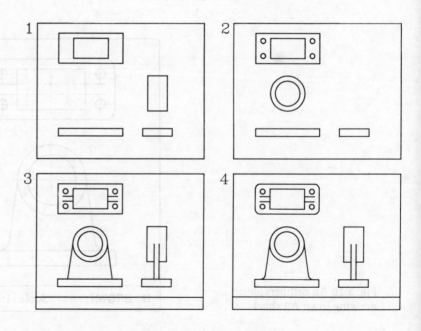

Fig. 3.11 Stages 1 to 4 in drawing Fig. 3.10

8. **Settings Line type**   Dialogue box settings:
        Center *point*
        Dialogue box **OK** *point*
9. **Settings Color**   Dialogue box settings:
        Green *point*
        Dialogue box **OK** *point*
    Draw centre lines (drawing 5 of Fig. 3.12)
10. **Settings Line type**   Dialogue box settings:
        Hidden *point*
        Dialogue box **OK** *point*
11. **Settings Color**   Dialogue box settings:
        Red *point*
        Dialogue box **OK** *point*
    Draw hidden detail lines (drawing 6 of Fig. 3.12)
12. **Settings Color**   Dialogue box settings:
        Cyan *point*
        Dialogue box **OK** *point*
    Add the text – third angle projection (drawing 7 of Fig. 3.12)
13. **Settings Color**   Dialogue box settings:
        Black *point*
        Dialogue box **OK** *point*
14. **Settings Text**   Dialogue box settings:
        Height 8 *Keyboard* OK
        Dialogue box **OK** *point*

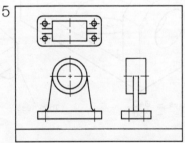

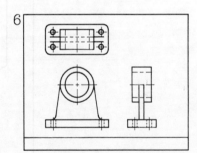

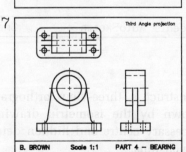

Fig. 3.12 Stages 5 to 7 in
drawing Fig. 3.10

Stages in constructing a
drawing with the aid of
AutoSketch

Add the text in the title box (drawing 7 of Fig. 3.12)

15. **File**   **Save as**   Dialogue box settings:

                    File name bracket   *Keyboard*
                    Dialogue box **OK** *point*

and the file is saved under the filename BRACKET.SKD.

Exercises

1. Construct the drawing Fig. 3.10 by following the procedure given above.
2. Construct a three-view orthographic projection of the item shown by the isometric drawing 2 of Fig. 3.13. Include all necessary centre and hidden detail lines. Do not include any dimensions.
3. Construct a three-view orthographic projection of the item shown by the isometric drawing 3 of Fig. 3.13. Include all necessary centre and hidden detail lines. Do not include any dimensions.

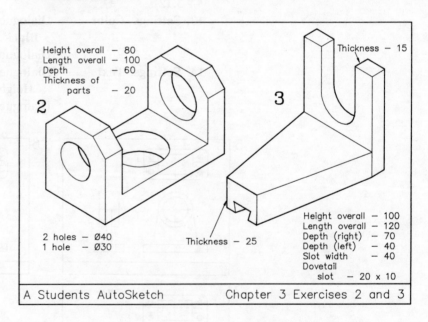

Fig. 3.13 Exercises 2 and 3

4. Construct a three-view orthographic projection of the item shown by the isometric drawing of Fig. 3.14. Include all necessary centre and hidden detail lines. Do not include any dimensions.

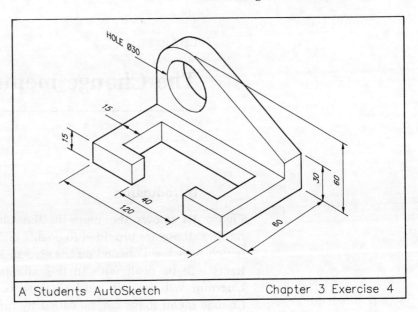

HOLE Ø30

15

15

30

60

120

40

80

60

A Students AutoSketch   Chapter 3 Exercise 4

Fig. 3.14 Exercise 4

CHAPTER 4

The Change menu

Introduction

Figure 4.1 shows the items in the **Change** menu. As its name implies, these are provided to enable changes to be made to objects which have been created on the screen. Not all of the **Change** menu items will be dealt with in this chapter – the items **Group** and **Ungroup** will be left until Chapter 6. Note that several of the **Change** menu items can be called by pressing function keys. Thus pressing F1 (function key F1) calls the menu item **Undo** into action. Figure 4.1 shows which of the menu items can be called by pressing function keys.

With the aid of CAD (Computer Aided Drawing) software such as AutoSketch, drawings can be produced much more quickly than they can be produced by hand methods of drawing. One of the major reasons for this is that there is rarely need to draw anything twice when using CAD software. The commands (menu items) in the **Change** menu demonstrate this clearly. Items such as **Erase**, **Move**, **Copy**, **Mirror** and **Rotate**, among others, allow the draughts-person to produce drawings, with the CAD motto in mind:

Never draw the same detail twice

Remember: in this book *point* = point at the detail with the AutoSketch pointer and press the device button.

The menu items Undo and Redo

Selecting and clicking on **Undo** (or pressing F1) undoes the last action performed by the operator, e.g., if a line had just been drawn, the line disappears from the screen; if part of a drawing has just been moved, the part returns to its original position. Continuous selection of **Undo** (or pressing F1) will eventually result in everything that has been added to the screen being deleted. When

The Change
pull–down menu

aw   Change   View

Undo	F1
Redo	F2
Erase	F3
Group	A9
Ungroup	A10
Move	F5
Copy	F6
Stretch	F7
Property	
Rotate	
Scale	
Mirror	
Break	F4
Chamfer	
Fillet	
Box Array	
Ring Array	

The Settings
pull–down menu

ist   Settings   Mea

Attach
Box Array
Chamfer
Color
Curve
Fillet
Grid
Layer
Limits
Line type
Part base
Pick
Property
Ring Array
Snap
Text
Units

Fig. 4.1 The Change and
Settings pull-down menus

this happens the word **Undo** in the menu changes to a greyish colour.

The item **Redo** reverses the last action of **Undo**. Continuous selection of **Redo** (or pressing F2) will eventually result in all objects which have been undone, reappearing on screen one after the other. When all has been redone, the word **Redo** in the menu will grey out.

Thus it is possible to **Undo** or **Redo** any drawing action taken by the operator. This is a valuable facility for immediately correcting errors, if they are spotted soon enough. Note that if both **Undo** and **Redo** are greyed out, neither item can be selected. Also, no part of a drawing which has been **Open**ed is affected by **Undo** or **Redo**. See page 89.

The menu item Erase

When **Erase** is selected (F3 will also call it) the AutoSketch arrow pointer changes to a small pointing hand, under the control of the pointing device. **Erase** can be operated in either of two ways:

1. If the hand is pointed at any single object on screen and the pick button of the pointing device pressed, the object disappears from the screen – it is erased. The prompt associated with the erasing of a single object is:

   Prompt   *Action*
   Erase Select object: *point* object disappears

2. If the hand is pointed anywhere on screen away from an object and the button of the pointing device pressed, AutoSketch assumes that a window is required to surround more than a single object. As the hand is repositioned on screen a window appears, its size controlled by the position of the hand pointer. When the button of the pointing device is again pressed, every object *completely* within the window will be erased. The window will either be made up of solid lines, or of dashed lines depending on whether the pointing hand is moved to the right or to the left (Fig. 4.2). A solid line window only selects items which lie totally within the window. A dashed line window selects all items through which its lines cross.

The prompts associated with the erasure of a group of objects are:

Prompt	Action
Erase Select object:	*point* at first corner
Erase Crosses/window corner:	*point* at second corner
	and the objects are erased.

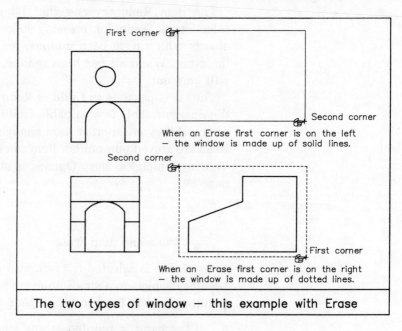

Fig. 4.2 Types of window

First corner

Second corner

When an Erase first corner is on the left
— the window is made up of solid lines.

Second corner

First corner

When an Erase first corner is on the right
— the window is made up of dotted lines.

The two types of window — this example with Erase

The menu item Move

The set of prompts for moving a single object are:

Prompt	Action
Move Select object:	*point* hand changes to arrow

Move From point:	*point* on the object
Move To point:	drag to new point *point*

and the object is moved to its new position (Fig. 4.3).

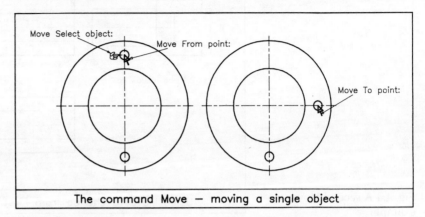

Move Select object:

Move From point:

Move To point:

The command Move — moving a single object

Fig. 4.3 An example of using the command Move

The prompts for moving a number of objects to another part of the screen are:

Prompt	*Action*
Move Select object:	*point* outside the area of the objects
Move Crosses/window corner:	move hand to second corner
	point hand changes to arrow *point*
Move From point:	
Move To point:	drag pointer to new position *point*

and the group of objects will be moved to the new position on screen. As the pointer is moved under the control of the pointing device, the objects will be dragged on screen in a ghosted form, allowing the required new position to be correctly placed.

Figure 4.4 shows the **Move** command used for changing the position of one of two views within a First-Angle orthographic projection to a new position to change the projection into Third Angle.

The menu item Copy

For a single object – the prompts are

Prompt	*Action*
Copy Select object:	*point* hand changes to arrow

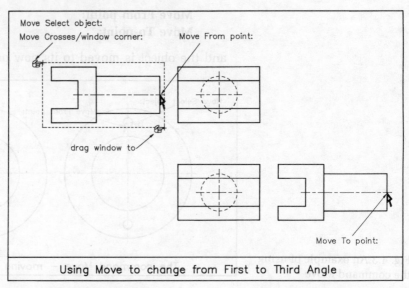

Fig. 4.4 A second Move
example

Using Move to change from First to Third Angle

Copy From point:	*point* on the object
Copy To point:	drag object to new point

and the object is copied to its new position.

For a group of objects:

Prompt	*Action*
Copy Select object:	*point*
Copy Crosses/window corner:	*point* drag hand acoss screen to form window *point*
Copy From point:	*point*
Copy To point:	drag to new point *point*

and the group of objects inside the window is copied in the new position. Figure 4.5 gives two examples of copying groups of objects from one position to another.

The menu item   Stretch

Stretch is only used with a window and prompts are:

Prompt	*Action*
Stretch First corner:	*point*
Stretch Crosses/window corner:	*point*
Stretch base:	*point*
Stretch Stretch to:	*point*

and the group of objects is stretched to its new shape. Figure 4.6

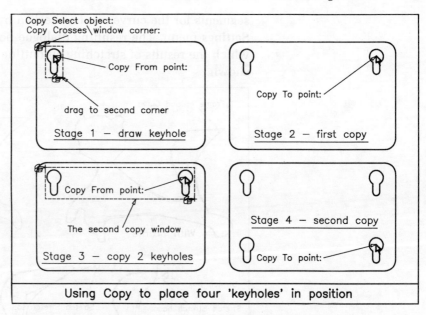

Stage 1 – draw keyhole

Stage 2 – first copy

Stage 3 – copy 2 keyholes

Stage 4 – second copy

Using Copy to place four 'keyholes' in position

Fig. 4.5 Examples of using
the command Copy

shows two examples of **Stretch** for changing the shape of a
drawing.

Note that circles cannot be stretched. If they form part of a
drawing, their size and shape is not changed and they will be
repositioned in a stretched drawing in their same size and in their
same relationship to other objects as in the pre-stretch drawing.

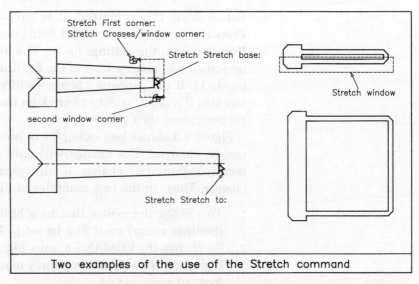

Stretch window

Two examples of the use of the Stretch command

Fig. 4.6 Two examples of
using the command Stretch

When **Stretch** is used with **Curve** from the **Draw** menu, if **Frame**
is on (**Assist** menu), the shape of the curve can be adjusted by
stretching at corners of the curve framework. The number of

segments for the curve can be checked by selecting **Curve** from the **Settings** menu. The resulting dialogue box is shown in Fig. 4.7, in which the results of stretching an outline drawn with **Curve** is also shown.

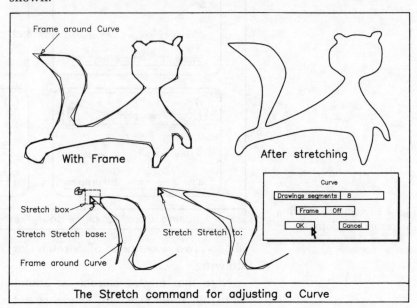

Fig. 4.7 An example of using Stretch on a Curve Frame

The menu item Property

Before using this command, it is advisable to check whether the **Property** facility for the object being changed is on – by selecting **Property** from the **Settings** menu. The dialogue box which appears on screen will show which of the facilities is on (tick against) or off (no tick). If the property change facility required is on select the box **OK**. If it is off, select and click on the rectangle to the left of the property, and then **OK**.

Figure 4.8 shows two examples of how the property of an object can be changed. The change will only take effect if the property required from the change is in operation at the time of the change. Thus, in the two examples of Fig. 4.8:

1. To change the centre line to a hidden detail line, **Line type** (**Settings** menu) must first be set to **Hidden**;
2. To change the ROMANS 8 units high font to ITALICC, 10 units high font, **Text** (**Settings** menu) must first be set for ITALICC font, 10 units height.

If a group of objects is included in a window, all the objects will change to their new properties, providing:

1. Each is set within the **Change property modes** dialogue box.
2. Each is set within its own dialogue box, e.g., line type, colour, text.

For a single object the prompts are:

Prompt	Action
Change property Select object:	*point*

For a group of objects:

Prompt	Action
Change property Crosses/ window corner:	enclose with a window point

Note: if **Layer** in the dialogue box is On, and another layer is the current layer, the object(s) whose properties are being changed will be changed to the current layer.

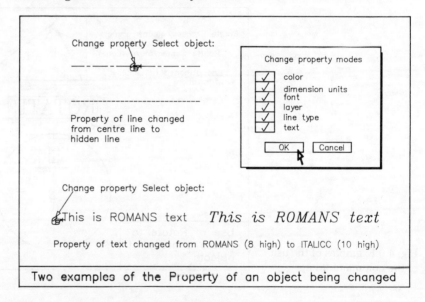

Fig. 4.8 Changing the Properties of objects

The menu item Rotate

Single objects or groups of objects can be repositioned at new angles of rotation with this command.

For a single object:

Prompt	Action
Rotate Select object:	*point*
Rotate Center of rotation:	*point*

a ghosted line attached to the chosen centre of rotation of the object (itself also ghosted) can be dragged around the centre of rotation to re-position the object into its required new position. When satisfied press the button of the pointing device and the object rotates to its new position.

For a group of objects:

Prompt	Action
Rotate Select object:	*point* first window corner
Rotate Crosses/window corner:	*point* on second corner
Rotate Center of rotation:	*point*

and the group of objects becomes ghosted with a ghosted rotation line to allow the group to be rotated to a new position around the centre of rotation. Figure 4.9 shows three examples of this command in action.

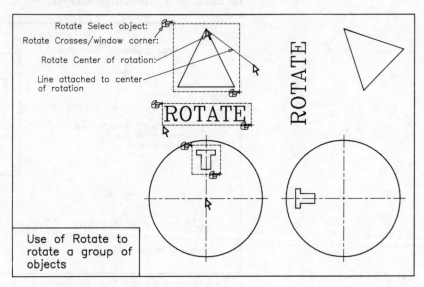

Fig. 4.9 Examples of the use of the command Rotate

The menu item Scale

To alter the size of a single object:

Prompt	Action
Scale Select object:	*point*
Scale Base point:	*point* and a ghosted line appears attached to the base point
Scale Second point:	drag scale to new position *point*

To alter the size of a group of objects:

Prompt Action

Scale Select object:	*point*
Scale Crosses/window corner:	*point* drag to other corner *point*
Scale Base point:	*point*
Scale Second point:	*drag scale line to new position point*

Figure 4.10 shows two examples of alteration of the scale of a drawing with this command. These examples show that either the whole drawing can be scaled or a small part of an overall drawing.

Notes

1. When an object or set of objects is being scaled, a figure giving the scale ratio is constantly being up-dated on the prompt line of the drawing editor screen. This figure shows scaling can take place only to one decimal point. As examples, it is not possible to scale to 0.25, but only to 0.2 or 0.3; scaling to 4.375 is not possible, but only to 4.3 or 4.4.
2. The figure on the prompt line showing the ratio of the scaling up-dates as the scaling line is dragged on the screen. Scaling by keying in a figure at the prompt line is not possible.

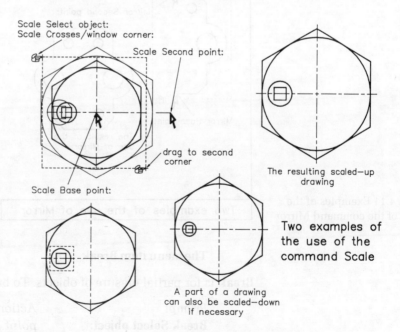

Scale Select object:
Scale Crosses/window corner:
Scale Second point:
drag to second corner
Scale Base point:
The resulting scaled—up drawing
Two examples of the use of the command Scale
A part of a drawing can also be scaled—down if necessary

Fig. 4.10 Examples of the use of the command Scale

The menu item Mirror

Two examples of the use of **Mirror** are included in Fig. 4.11. When constructing a drawing which is symmetrical about either one or several axes, the production of the complete drawing can be speeded up with the aid of **Mirror**. To use the command, first draw one-half (or one-quarter) of the complete drawing and then mirror that half (or quarter) around the lines of symmetry. The prompts for producing the drawings of Fig. 4.11 are:

Prompt	Action
Mirror Select object:	*point*
Mirror Crosses/window corner:	*point* drag to other corner *point*
Mirror Base point:	*point*
Mirror Second point:	*point*

and the selected objects are mirrored as required.

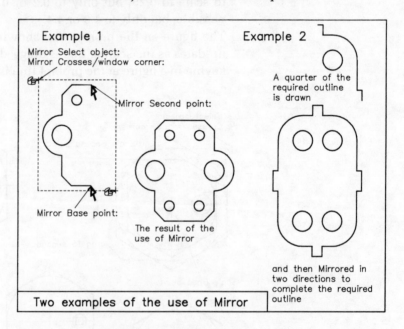

Fig. 4.11 Examples of the use of the command Mirror

The menu item Break

Break is for partial erasure of objects. To break a single object:

Prompt	Action
Break Select object:	*point* the object becomes dotted
Break First break point:	*point*

Break Second break point: *point* and the object breaks between the two points

To break a group of objects:

Prompt	Action
Break Select object:	*point*
Break Crosses/window corner:	drag to second corner *point* (only one of the objects becomes dotted)
Break First break point:	*point* (first dotted line)
Break Second break point:	*point* (another object becomes dotted)
Break First break point:	*point*
Break Second break point:	*point* (another object becomes dotted)

and so on until all objects within the window which are to be broken are broken.

Notes

1. Figure 4.12 shows the breaking of a line and the breaking of a circle. Note that in circles the second break point must be anti-clockwise from the first. Failure to observe this will result in a break of the wrong part of the circle.

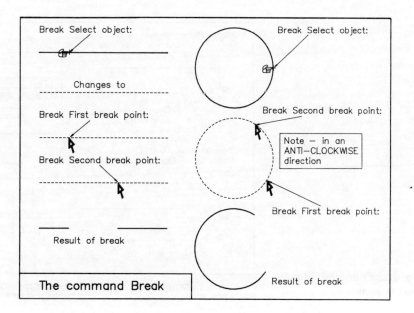

Fig. 4.12 Examples of the use of Break

2. Breaking a group of objects within a window may be of use when hatching a sectional view with the aid of Box Array. But remember that the outline of the area being hatched may fall within the window and thus become subject to the Break command. See page 122.

The menu item Chamfer

Chamfer is another menu item which can only be used with the aid of the same item from the **Settings** menu. Figure 4.13 shows details of the forming of a chamfer from unit sizes keyed into the **Chamfer** dialogue box from the **Settings** menu.

The prompts follow the form:

Prompt	Action
Chamfer Select line(s):	point
Chamfer Select second line:	point

and the chamfer automatically forms to the unit sizes keyed into the **Chamfer** dialogue box.

Notes

1. If a different size of chamfer is required, the **Chamfer** dialogue box must be called and the new units keyed in.
2. Chamfers can only be formed between lines.

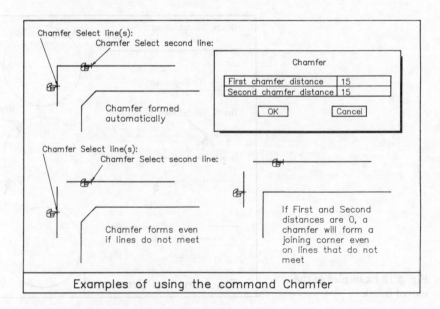

Fig. 4.13 Examples of the use of Chamfer

3. Chamfers can be formed on lines at any angle to each other.
4. To form a precise join between two lines, set both Chamfer distances to 0 in the dialogue box.

The menu item Fillet

Fillets are formed in a similar manner to chamfers, except that only one figure needs to be keyed into the **Fillet** dialogue box from the **Settings** menu. See Fig. 4.14.

The prompts are:

Prompt	Action
Fillet Select line(s):	point
Fillet Select second line:	point

and the fillet forms.

Notes

1. Fillets will form for two lines which do not meet, even when the lines are outside the limits of the fillet radius.
2. If the fillet radius is set at 0 a sharp corner join can be formed between two lines with the aid of the **Fillet** command.
3. Fillets can be formed between lines at any angle to each other.

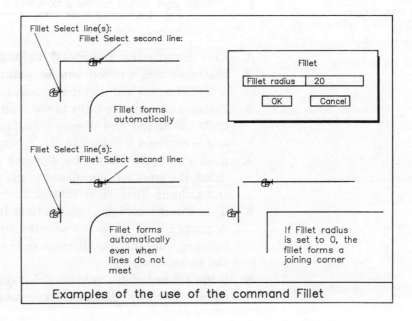

Fig. 4.14 Examples of the use of Fillet

The menu item Box Array

This command produces multiple copies of objects or groups of objects in rows and columns. Figure 4.15 is an example – a drawing composed of a polygon containing a small rectangle has been copied in rows and columns in a Box Array. The distances between the rows and between the columns, together with the number of rows and number of columns, must first be keyed in the **Box Array Settings** dialogue box selected from the **Settings** menu. In this dialogue box:

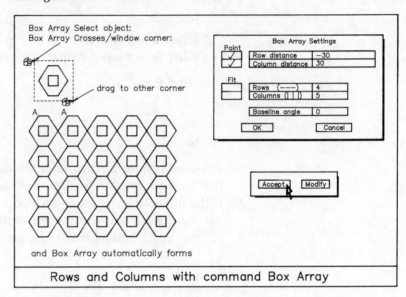

Fig. 4.15 Example of the use of Box Array

1. **Row** distances are horizontal, **Column** distances vertical.
2. Distances are between similar points on the object(s) in an array. Thus the column distance AA in Fig. 4.15 is 30 units.
3. Distances are in +ve units to the right and upwards and in −ve units to the left and downwards, i.e. they correspond to +ve and −ve x and y values in the x,y coordinate system.
4. If all **Point** and **Fit** in the dialogue rectangles are empty (no ticks), the array will be spaced to the units in the **Row** distance and **Column** distance rectangles.
5. If the **Point** rectangles contain ticks (on), then the whole array is contained in distances selected by pointing on the screen. Pointing only the row distance or the column distance or both can be selected.
6. If the **Fit** rectangles contain ticks, the *whole* array is fitted in either the row distance, the column distance, or both,

depending on whether the row fit the column fit, or both are ticked;

Figure 4.16 shows the differences between these settings.

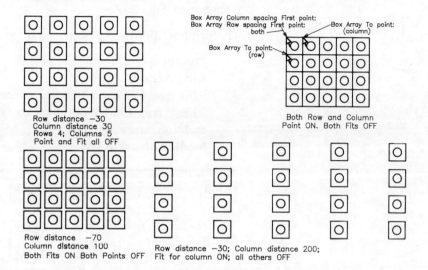

Fig. 4.16 A second example of Box Array

The prompts follow a pattern such as:

Prompt	Action
Box Array Select object:	*point*
Box Array Crosses/window corner:	drag window *point*

the box array forms on screen; a small dialogue box appears with

Accept Modify	select whichever is appropriate.

The menu item Ring Array

This functions in much the same way as does **Box Array**, except that the array is formed in a circle around a selected centre point. Figure 4.17 shows two examples. In the upper of these two, the items in the array have been rotated as they have been copied – note the tick against **Rotate items as copied** in the dialogue box. In the lower example the items have not been rotated as copied – no tick in the rectangle alongside **Rotate items as copied**.

Notes

1. If **Point** is on (ticked) the centre point of the array is chosen by

pointing the AutoSketch arrow at the required centre.

2. If **Point** is off (no tick) then the centre point must be typed in the box for the X and Y coordinates.

3. The **rotate items as copied** rectangle from the dialogue box is shown in Fig. 4.17.

The prompts follow a pattern such as:

Prompt	Action
Ring Array:	*point* and drag window
Ring Array Crosses/window corner:	
Ring Array Center point of array:	*point*

and the array appears on screen with the small **Accept Modify** dialogue box.

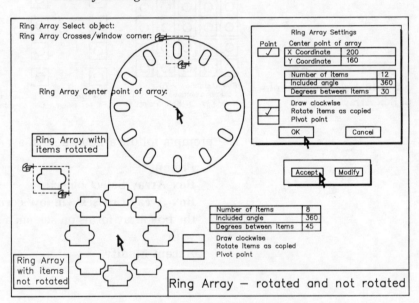

Fig. 4.17 Examples of the use of Ring Array

Note: a **Ring Array** can be constructed within part of a circle, if a figure other than 360 is keyed in to the **Included angle** detail in the dialogue box for **Ring Array**. Thus a Ring Array for a semi-circle can be achieved by keying in 180 at the **Included angle** rectangle – or indeed any other figure that is desired.

Exercises

1. Draw the plan of the single room shown in Fig. 4.18 to the dimensions given. Then **Copy** (or **Box Array**) the single room to produce the set of rooms in a line. Complete your drawing by adding the two end lines on right and left.

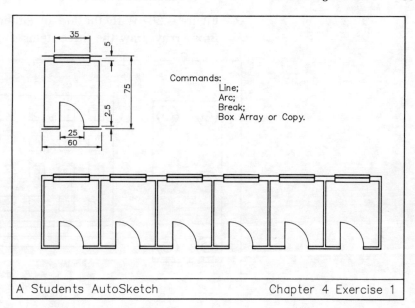

Fig. 4.18 Exercise 1

2. Draw in Third Angle projection to the given dimensions the three-view orthographic projection given in Fig. 4.19. Outline lines should be solid black; hidden detail should be red hidden; centre lines should be green center; text should be romans, 6 high in cyan. Do not include any dimensions.

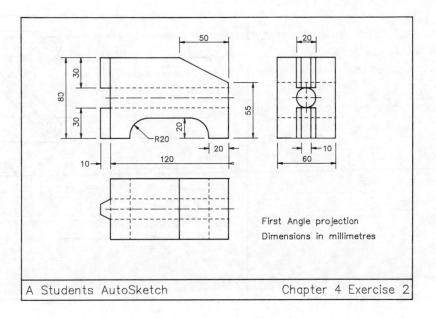

Fig. 4.19 Exercise 2

3. Figure 4.20. With the aid of either the menu items **Copy** or **Box Array** draw the three items shown.

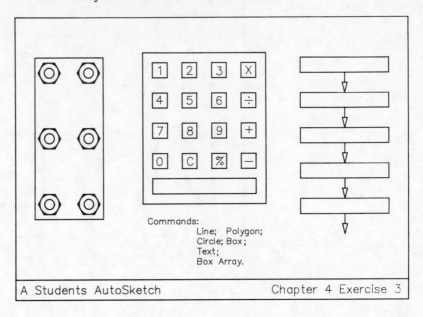

Commands:
Line; Polygon;
Circle; Box;
Text;
Box Array.

A Students AutoSketch   Chapter 4 Exercise 3

Fig. 4.20 Exercise 3

4. Figure 4.21. Working to any suitable dimensions, construct the four drawings shown, using the commands (menu items) given with the drawings. Use solid black outlines and green centre lines.

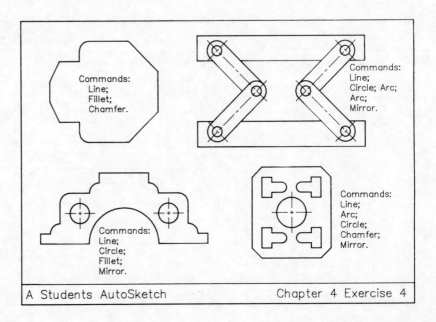

Commands:
Line;
Fillet;
Chamfer.

Commands:
Line;
Circle; Arc;
Arc;
Mirror.

Commands:
Line;
Circle;
Fillet;
Mirror.

Commands:
Line;
Arc;
Circle;
Chamfer;
Mirror.

A Students AutoSketch   Chapter 4 Exercise 4

Fig. 4.21 Exercise 4

5. Construct each of the three drawing of Fig. 4.22, each on its own A3 sheet file. Construct each drawing as large as the screen allows. Work with the commands given with each of the three drawings. Work with black solid outlines, green centre lines and cyan text.

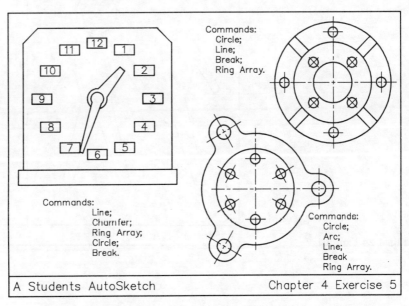

Fig. 4.22 Exercise 5

6. Draw each of the three items shown in Fig. 4.23, working to any suitable size. Then practise with the command **Stretch** on each of the outlines.

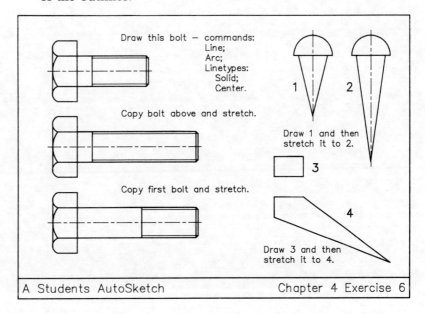

Fig. 4.23 Exercise 6

7. With the aid of **Mirror** draw the two outlines in Fig. 4.24. Use solid black outlines and green centre lines.

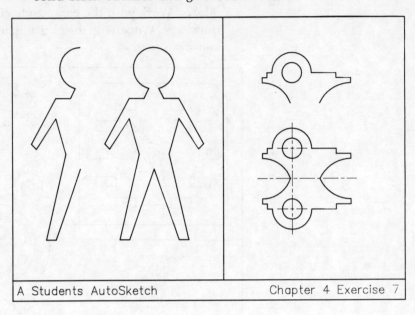

A Students AutoSketch   Chapter 4 Exercise 7

Fig. 4.24 Exercise 7

CHAPTER 5

The View menu

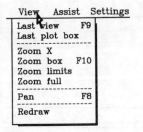

Fig. 5.1 The View pull-down
menu

The items

As Fig. 5.1 shows, the items in the **View** menu are **Zoom**
commands, except for **Last plot box**, **Pan** and **Redraw**.

The menu item Last view

When this item is selected, the screen regenerates and redraws to
the previous Zoom screen. **Last view** can also be called by pressing
the function key F9.

The menu item Last Plot box

Selecting this item causes the last plot box used when plotting to
appear on the screen. See Chapter 7.

The menu item Zoom X

When **Zoom X** is selected, a dialogue box appears on the screen –
Fig. 5.2. Pointing at the rectangle to the right of **Magnification
factor** highlights it. The required scaling figures can then be keyed
into the rectangle. These may be to scale the screen drawing up or
down in size, either for an enlargement or a reduction of the
drawing on screen. Figure 5.3 shows the result when the
Magnification factor 1.25 is keyed in and **OK** selected on the
dialogue box.

The menu item Zoom box

This is selected either by pointing at the item or by pressing key
F10 – Fig. 5.4. This is probably the zoom command you will be
using most frequently. The following prompts appear at the prompt
line:

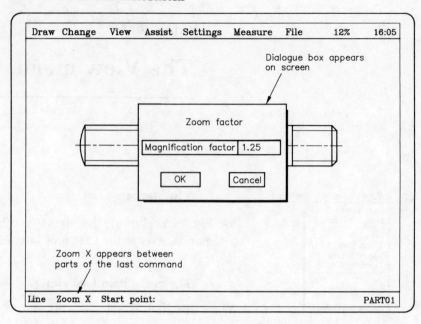

Fig. 5.2 The Zoom X
dialogue box

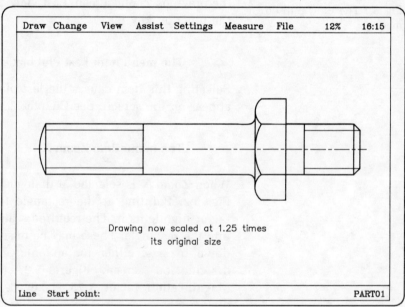

Fig. 5.3 A drawing Zoomed
to a stated X scale

Prompt	Action
Zoom box First corner:	*point*
Zoom box Second corner:	*point*

and the area within the selected window is enlarged to fill the
whole screen. Figure 5.5 shows the result of zooming the window
of Fig. 5.4. Note that **Zoom box** can be applied to extremely small

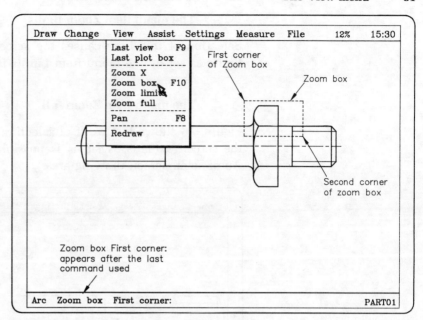

Fig. 5.4 An example of the use of Zoom box

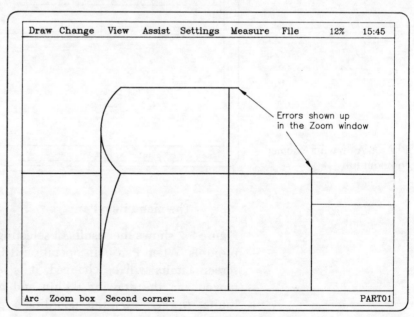

Fig. 5.5 The screen after the Zoom box of Fig. 5.4

areas of the screen, in which parts of a drawing covering just a small area of the screen can be re-displayed to fill the whole screen. **Zoom box** is a powerful command, allowing accurate areas of construction or correction in very small areas of the screen.

The menu item Zoom limits

Selection of this item causes the screen to revert to the original limits as set by the menu item **Limits** from the **Se**ttings **menu.**

The menu item Zoom full

Figure 5.6 shows the result of selecting this item. The drawing on the screen extends as far as is possible to the boundaries of the AutoSketch screen drawing area.

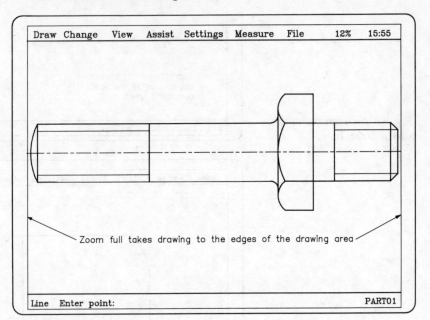

Draw Change   View   Assist Settings Measure   File   12%   15:55

Zoom full takes drawing to the edges of the drawing area

Line   Enter point: PART01

Fig. 5.6 A drawing Zoomed to Zoom full

The menu item Pan

Figure 5.7 shows the results of selecting this item and following its prompts. When **Pan** is in operation it is important to note that the screen **Limits** will be changed. It is not just the drawing that is moved, but the drawing within and including its x,y coordinate limits. In Fig. 5.7, the coordinate point $x,y = (0,0)$ will be somewhere below the screen when the **Pan** has been carried out. Thus if **Zoom limits** is called after a **Pan**, the screen will revert to its original screen limits.

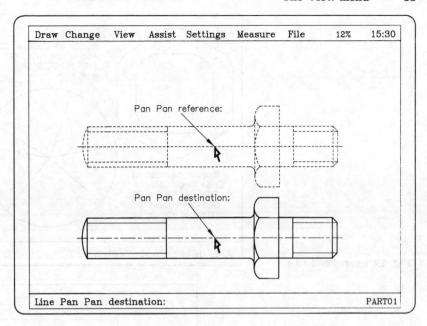

Fig. 5.7 An example of the use of Pan

The menu item Redraw

When **Redraw** is selected, the screen goes blank for a very short time and its contents then regenerate. When **Redraw** is called, the screen is refreshed and parts of the construction which may have been partly obliterated, e.g., by a nearby erasure, show up clearly on screen again.

Exercises

The following exercises are intended to allow the reader to revise work from earlier chapters. However as the following exercises are worked, it will be found there is a constant need to use the **Zoom** commands to ensure accurate constructions.

1. Construct drawing 1 of Fig. 5.8.
2. Construct drawing 2 of Fig. 5.8. This drawing demonstrates how the segments of a pie chart could be constructed in AutoSketch.
3. Construct drawing 3 of Fig. 5.8. Sizes not given are left to the reader's judgement.
4. Construct the outline of the SHELF BRACKET shown in Fig. 5.9. Dimensions not given are left to your own judgement.
5. Working in Third-Angle orthographic projection construct accurate three-view projection of the given PIN SUPPORT,

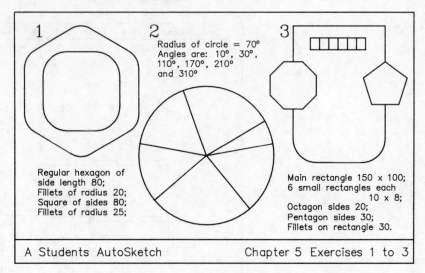

Fig. 5.8 Exercises 1 to 3

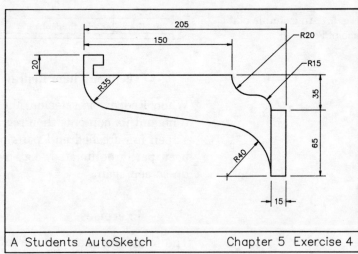

Fig. 5.9 Exercise 4

Fig. 5.10. Do not include any dimensions.

6. Figure 5.11 is a plan of a single workshop unit, which is to be built as one of a side-by-side set of six similar units. The only difference between the units is that the pairs of WCs will be placed as shown in the outline drawing Fig. 5.12 when the building has been completed. Copy Fig. 5.11 to a suitable scale and then with the menu items **Copy** and/or **Box Array**, complete the required complete drawing.

7. Two drawings of building construction details from the unit workshop (Fig. 5.11) are given in Fig. 5.13. Working to sizes of your own choice, copy the two given drawings.

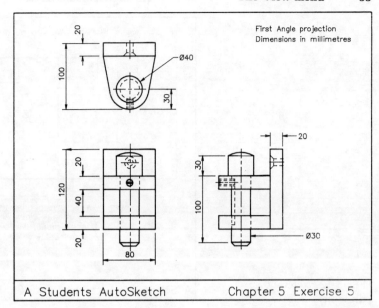

Fig. 5.10 Exercise 5

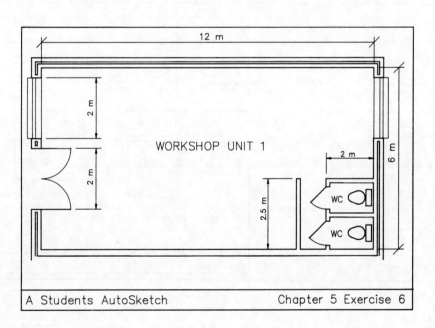

Fig. 5.11 Exercise 6

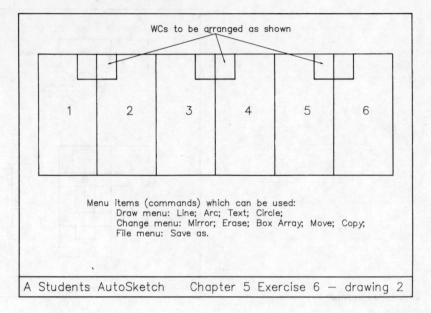

Fig. 5.12 Exercise 6,
drawing 2

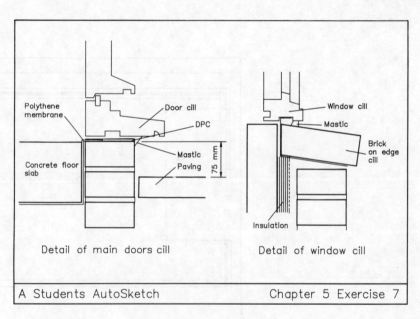

Fig. 5.13 Exercise 7

8. Construct the TAB WASHER shown in Fig. 5.14. The left-hand drawing shows how the drawing can be started. Use **Ring Array** to complete the drawing.

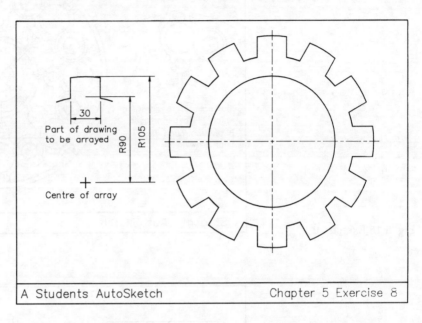

30

Part of drawing
to be arrayed

R90 R105

Centre of array

A Students AutoSketch   Chapter 5 Exercise 8

Fig. 5.14 Exercise 8

9. Figure 5.15. Here is a much more difficult **Ring Array**. If you feel you can attempt it, by all means do so, but this drawing requires a good degree of skill with AutoSketch. **Zoom** will have to be frequently called to ensure accurate construction. The drawing on the left shows how to start the drawing. Use your own judgement for sizes.

10. Try drawing the optical illusion – drawing 10 of Fig. 5.16. The shading was drawn with the aid of **Box Array** and **Break**.

11. Drawing 11 of Fig. 5.16 represents light-emitting diode (LED) figures from a clock. When drawing these, you will find that some experimentation is required to obtain correct angles. When the three given figures have been drawn, attempt others of the same design.

12. Drawing 12 of Fig. 5.16. Construct the given road sign. Find examples of other road signs to construct.

13. The given drawing 13 is a symbol of a fan from a car dashboard. Construct the symbol and find others which you can draw.

14. Copy drawing 14 of Fig. 5.16.

15. Two views of a toy farm machine are given in Fig. 5.17. Copy the two views and add a plan view.

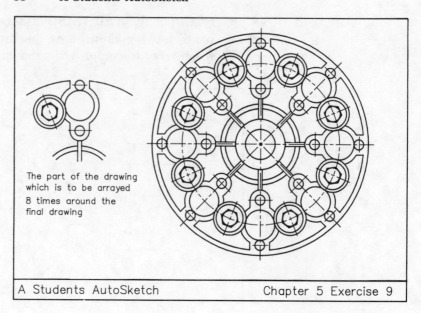

Fig. 5.15 Exercise 9

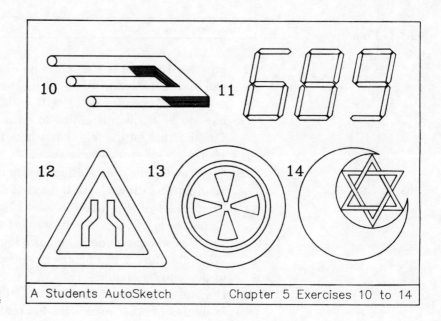

Fig. 5.16 Exercises 10 to 14

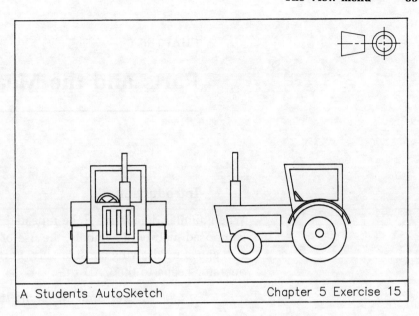

A Students AutoSketch   Chapter 5 Exercise 15

Fig. 5.17 Exercise 15

CHAPTER 6

Parts and the Measure menu

Introduction

When similar details are to be repeated in a drawing or when it is composed mainly of symbols, the use of the **Draw** menu item **Part** will speed up drawing considerably. **Part** helps in ensuring that the operator keeps to the CAD rule:

Never draw the same thing twice

Constructing a drawing for a Part file

There are four stages in the construction of a **Part**. These are:

1. draw the **Part**;
2. **Group** the objects making up the **Part**;
3. select a **Part base**;
4. save the drawing as a file.

Notes

1. If the objects making up a **Part** drawing are not grouped, the **Part** cannot be scaled in size or moved easily around the screen as if it were a single object;
2. If a **Part base** point is not selected, the coordinate point x,y = (0,0) is taken as being the **Part base**. This can cause difficulty when moving the **Part**.
3. Either select a **Part base** with **Snap** operating, or ensure that **Attach** from the **Assist** menu is on (ticked). When positioning symbols on screen from **Part** files, they must be accurately placed. Otherwise it is very difficult to add joining lines between symbols with any degree of accuracy.
4. When saving a drawing as a **Part** file, the whole screen is saved. Because of this items such as a symbol being saved as a **Part** file must be the only item drawn on the screen.

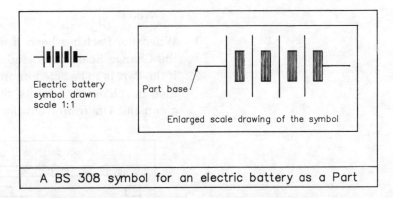

Fig. 6.1 An electric symbol for filing as a Part

An example of a Part

A British Standards drawing of a symbol of an electrical battery is given in Fig. 6.1. To make a **Part** file for the battery drawing:

Menu	Item	Action
1. **File**	**Open**	A3SHEET *Keyboard OK*
2.		draw the symbol (Fig. 6.1)
3. **Change**	**Group**	window the symbol
4. **Change**	**Group**	a second time
5. **Settings**	**Part base**	Dialogue box settings **Set by pointing** *point* (Fig. 6.2)

Note: The Part base of the battery is indicated in Fig. 6.1

6. **File**	**Save as**	BATTERY *Keyboard button*

Fig. 6.2 The Part base dialogue box

and the symbol drawing is saved as an AutoSketch drawing file with the filename battery.skd.

Inserting a Part into a drawing

To insert the **Part** BATTERY in position within another drawing:

Menu	Item	Action
1. **Draw**	**Part**	Dialogue box settings **File name** BATTERY *point* (Fig. 6.3) Dialogue box *OK*

2. battery symbol appears on screen held at its Part base on the end of the pointer arrow;
3. drag the symbol to the position required on screen and press pointer button. Symbol is inserted on screen.

Notes

1. When the **Part** has been inserted, its size can be altered with the **Change Scale** command.
2. If the **Part** is to be acted upon by the **Stretch** menu item, it must first be changed into its original drawing objects with the command **Ungroup** from the **Change** menu.

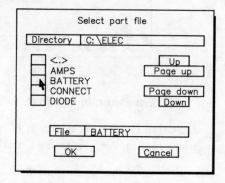

Fig. 6.3 The Part dialogue box

Parts libraries

Many types of drawing include symbols. Examples are:

1. engineering drawings – conventional drawings of bolts, nuts, washers, other fittings, dimensioning symbols for tolerances, etc.;
2. electrical and electronics circuit drawings symbols;
3. pneumatics and hydraulics circuit drawings symbols;
4. computer gate circuits symbols;
5. building drawings – details such as windows, doors.

Sets (libraries) of such symbols can run into hundreds of files. Libraries of symbol files can be built up as the need for them arises. Because so many files may be involved, save them on their own discs, preferably in separate directories – one (or more) for each type of symbol. Thus files could be organised in directories such as *eng* for engineering detail, *elec* for electrical symbols, *pneu* for pneumatic symbols.

Examples of drawings from Part files

A number of electrical and electronics circuit diagram symbols saved for use as **Part** files are given in Fig. 6.4. Note that it is quite impossible, in a book of this size, to show all electric/electronic

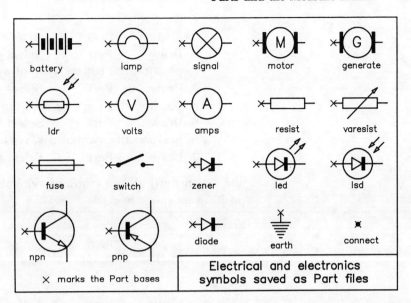

Fig. 6.4 Electrical and electronics symbols saved as Part files

symbols – there are thousands of them. In Fig. 6.4 the **Part base** points are indicated with crosses. These are not saved with the files. They are shown to record in a drawing the positions of the insertion points when the symbols are to be added to a circuit drawing.

Figure 6.5 illustrates a sequence for building up a circuit drawing from **Part** files.

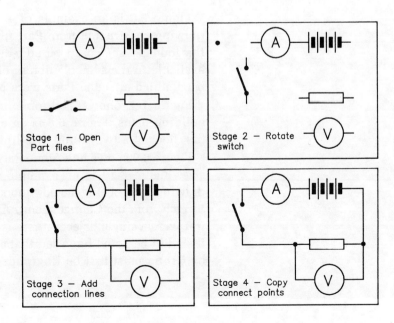

Fig. 6.5 Stages in constructing a simple electrical circuit from Part files

Stage 1

Menu	Item	Action	
1. **Draw**	**Part**	**Select part file BATTERY**	OK
2. position the battery symbol on screen			
3. **Draw**	**Part**	**Select part file AMPS**	OK
4. position the amps symbol on screen			
5. **Draw**	**Part**	**Select part file SWITCH**	OK
6. position the symbol SWITCH on screen			
7. **Draw**	**Part**	**Select part file RESIST**	**OK**

and so on until all the required symbols are in their approximate position on the screen.

Stage 2

Menu	Item	Action
Change	**Rotate**	rotate the switch symbol

Stage 3

Menu	Item	Action
Draw	**Line**	add connecting lines between the symbols. If necessary also:
Change	**Move**	re-position symbols

Stage 4

Menu	Item	Action
Change	**Copy**	copy the symbols CONNECT at conductor jointing points.

Figure 6.6 is an example of a more complex electronics circuit drawing constructed from **Part** files. If necessary, symbols such as the loudspeaker could be added to the circuit by drawing if not available in the symbols library of files. The component sizes have been added after the Parts were positioned.

Figure 6.7 shows part of a library of **Part** files for drawing building plans. Figure 6.8 is an example of a building plan of the first floor of a two-storey dwelling drawn from these Part files.

Figure 6.9 shows how some **Part** files can be adapted in scale and size. Figure 6.10 is an example of two Part files inserted into a drawing after being acted upon by the menu items **Scale** and **Stretch** from the **Change** menu. A **Part** can be changed by **Scale** as if it were a single object – there is no need to place it in a window. It should be noted however, that a **Part** which has been acted upon by **Group** must first be **Ungroup**ed before it can be **Stretch**ed.

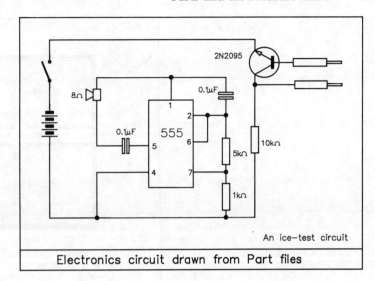

Fig. 6.6 An example of an electronics circuit constructed from Part files

Electronics circuit drawn from Part files

An ice-test circuit

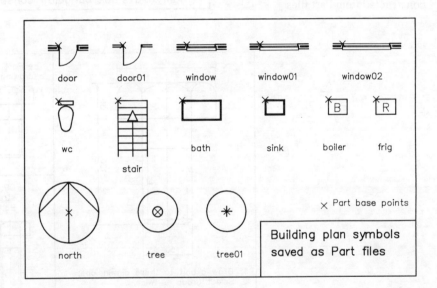

Fig. 6.7 Building plan symbols saved as Part files

Building plan symbols saved as Part files

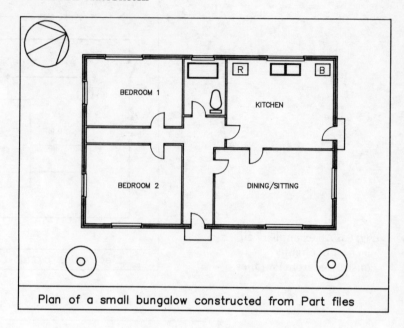

Fig. 6.8 A building plan
constructed from Part files

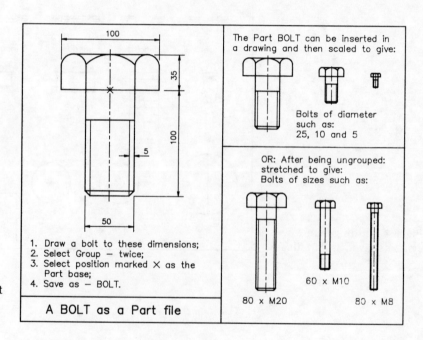

Fig. 6.9 Details of how a Part
file of a bolt can be scaled
and/or stretched

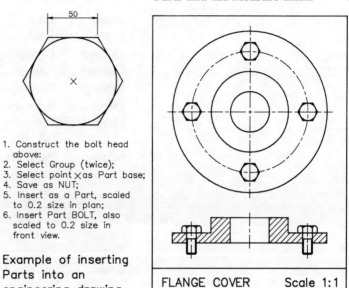

1. Construct the bolt head above:
2. Select Group (twice);
3. Select point ✕ as Part base;
4. Save as NUT;
5. Insert as a Part, scaled to 0.2 size in plan;
6. Insert Part BOLT, also scaled to 0.2 size in front view.

Example of inserting Parts into an engineering drawing

FLANGE COVER   Scale 1:1

Fig. 6.10 Inserting Part file drawings into an engineering drawing

Dimensions from Parts

Dimensions to British Standard 308 specification can be added to a drawing from purpose-designed **Part** files. Draw and save four files for dimension arrows. (Figure 6.11.) Follow the procedure:

Menu	Item	Action
File	**Open**	select A3SHEET
Settings	**Color**	red

◄ Arrow LEFT

► Arrow RIGHT

Λ Arrow TOP

V Arrow BOTTOM

The four arrows drawn to an enlarged scale

Line P(5,10)

Part base

Line P(5,350)

Details of arrows

100

110

Ø40

45°

An example of dimensioning from Parts

Dimensioning from Parts

Fig. 6.11 Using Part files for dimensioning a drawing

Draw	**Line**	draw line P(5,10)
Draw	**Line**	draw line P(5,350)
Change	**Group**	window the two lines
Change	**Group**	a second time
Settings	**Part base**	*point*
File	**Save as**	RIGHT *Keyboard button*
Change	**Rotate**	*point* at the part base; rotate through 180°
Settings	**Part base**	*point*
File	**Save as**	LEFT

Repeat for TOP and BOTTOM arrow files, i.e. rotate 90°.

To draw dimensions with these Part files

	Menu	Item	Action
1.	**Settings**	**Color**	red
2.	**Draw**	**Line**	draw dimension and extension lines
3.	**Draw**	**Part**	select LEFT from file dialogue box
4.	Drag LEFT arrow on to the left end of the dimension line
5.	Repeat with RIGHT arrow
6.	**Draw**	**Text**	add figures of dimension

Notes

1. The same procedure can be followed for a vertical dimension with TOP and BOTTOM arrow files.
2. If an aligned or a leader dimension is required, any one of the four arrows can be rotated in line with the sloping dimension line.
3. Similarly, arrows for an angle dimension can be rotated at the ends of the dimension arcs.

Fig. 6.12 The Measure pull-down menu

The Measure menu

The menu items in **Measure** include not only measuring command but also automatic dimensioning items – Fig. 6.12. Methods for non-automatic dimensioning have been described above using the **Part** command. The dimensioning items in **Measure** can only be used for automatic dimensioning. The measuring items are of value for checking details already added to a drawing, such as length, angle, coordinate position, layer, size of text, etc.

The menu item Distance

When **Distance** is selected by pointing at the word in the **Measure** menu, prompts appear in succession on the prompt line asking for first and second distance points. When these have been selected a dialogue box appears with a statement of the required distance stated as shown in Fig. 6.13.

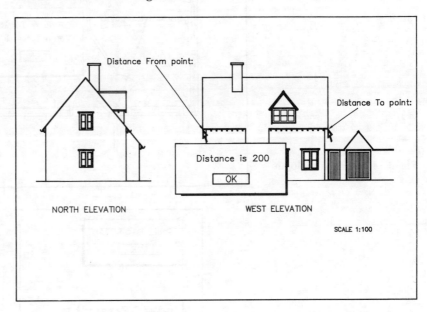

Fig. 6.13 The Distance dialogue box

The menu item Area

Upon selecting **Area**, a prompt **Area First perimeter point:** appears at the prompt line. When the point has been selected, the prompt changes to **Area Next point:** and when that has been chosen this prompt is repeated. The prompting continues until the **First perimeter point** is selected a second time. Then a dialogue box such as that shown in Fig. 6.14 appears giving not only the perimeter length, but also the area inside the chosen perimeter.

Note that the actual perimeter and area sizes must be calculated from the figures shown in relation to the scale at which the drawing has been constructed.

The menu items Angle, Point and Bearing

These three items each with its own dialogue box (Fig. 6.15) will state the angle of two lines to each other in degrees, the bearing in degrees of one point on the screen to another, and the x,y coordinates of a selected point on the screen.

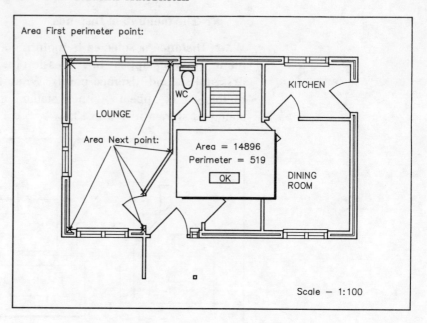

Fig. 6.14 The Area dialogue box

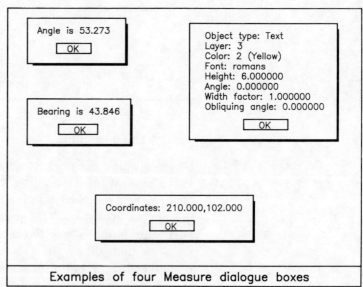

Fig. 6.15 Examples of four Measure dialogue boxes

The menu item Property

When this item is selected, the prompt line shows:

Show properties Select object:

Upon selection of an object, a dialogue box such as shown in Fig. 6.15 appears containing information about the various properties of the selected object – in this case some text.

The Dimension menu items

The dimensioning items in the **Measure** menu – **Angle dimension**, **Align dimension**, **Horiz dimension**, **Vert dimension** – are all completely automatic. This means that all that is required is to follow the prompts at the prompt line. Then the complete dimension appears on the drawing. The dimensioning prompts take the form:

Menu item Angle dimension

Prompt	Action
Angular dimension Select first line:	point
Angular dimension Select second line:	point
Angular dimension Dimension line arc location:	point

and the angle in degrees automatically appears.

Menu item Align dimension

Prompt	Action
Aligned dimension Points to dimension:	point
Angular dimension To point:	point
Angular dimension Dimension line location:	point

and the angle dimension automatically appears.

Menu item Horiz dimension

Prompt	Action
Horizontal dimension Points to dimension:	point
Horizontal dimension To point:	point
Horizontal dimension Dimension line location:	point

and the horizontal dimension automatically appears.

Menu item Vert dimension

Prompt	Action
Vertical dimension Points to dimension:	point
Vertical dimension To point:	point
Vertical dimension Dimension line location:	point

and the vertical dimension automatically appears.

Notes

1. The settings for the item **Text** from the **Settings** menu determine the following details when AutoSketch automatic dimensioning is in operation:
   (a) font style of dimension figures;
   (b) length of dimension arrows;
   (c) gap between outline and dimension extension line;
   (d) extension of dimension extension line beyond dimension line.

2. The setting for the item **Units** from the **Settings** menu determines the type of dimension which will appear with AutoSketch automatic dimensioning – either **Decimal** or **Architectural**. If **Decimal** units are chosen, the number of **digits** selected in the **Units** dialogue box control the number of digits appearing after the decimal point in the dimensions.

3. Each dimension is a **Group** (see page 78). Any attempt to erase any part of a dimension results in the whole dimension being erased.

4. When inserting vertical dimensions, if the lower point is selected before the upper, the dimension will be readable from the right-hand side of the drawing.

Figures 6.16 and 6.17 show the form taken by AutoSketch automatic dimensioning from items in the **Measure** menu.

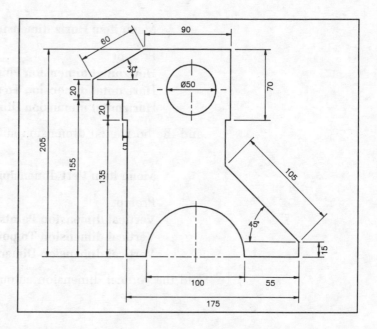

Fig. 6.16 Examples of automatic dimensioning in AutoSketch

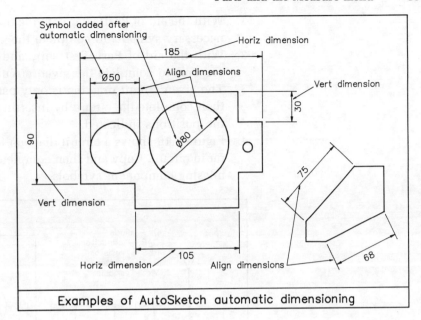

Fig. 6.17 A second example of AutoSketch automatic dimensioning

Exercises

The drawings for Exercises 1 to 3 are given in Fig. 6.18. From details given in Fig. 6.4 construct the necessary symbols to save as **Part** files to answer Exercises 1 to 4.

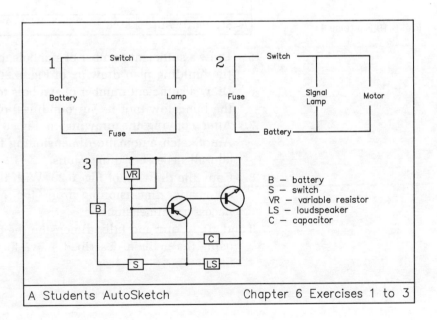

Fig. 6.18 Exercises 1 to 3

1. With the aid of **Part**, after copying the given drawing, insert the necessary symbols to complete the given circuit.
2. With the aid of **Part**, first copy and then insert the necessary symbols to complete the given circuit.
3. The given circuit drawing is only partly complete. Copy it and then complete the circuit by inserting the necessary symbols in the positions indicated.
4. Figure 6.19 shows a circuit diagram for a very simple transistor radio circuit. Copy and then complete the circuit by adding the missing component symbols.

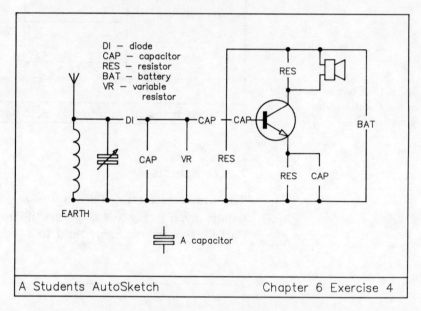

Fig. 6.19 Exercise 4

5. Draw a sufficient number of symbols to copy and then complete the building plan drawing of Fig. 6.20.
6. Draw a sufficient number of symbols to draw a building plan of the bungalow (not its surroundings) of Fig. 6.21.
7. After copying the drawing in Fig. 6.22, with the aid of the AutoSketch automatic dimensioning from the **Measure** menu, add all necessary dimensions.
8. Copy the drawing of Fig. 6.23. With the aid of the AutoSketch automatic dimensioning from the **Measure** menu, add all necessary dimensions.

9 and 10. Copy and fully dimension the two drawings of Fig. 6.24 using the method described above for dimensioning with **Part** files.

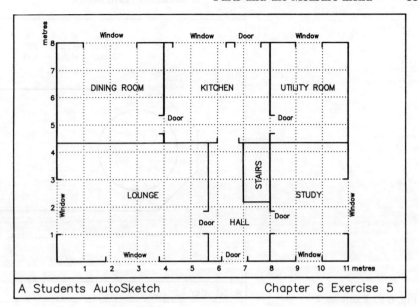

Fig. 6.20 Exercise 5

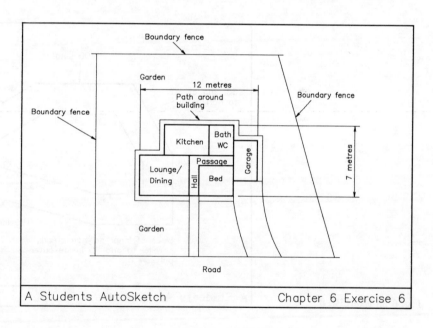

Fig. 6.21 Exercise 6

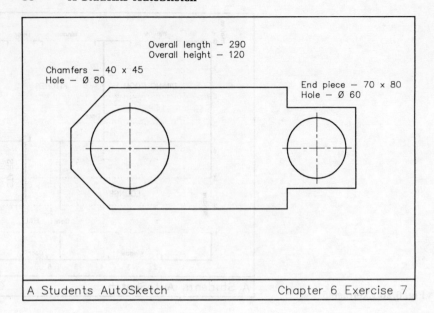

Overall length — 290
Overall height — 120

Chamfers — 40 x 45
Hole — Ø 80

End piece — 70 x 80
Hole — Ø 60

A Students AutoSketch   Chapter 6 Exercise 7

Fig. 6.22 Exercise 7

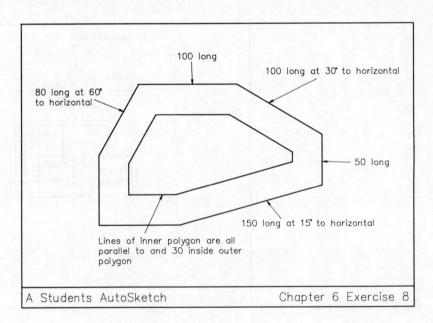

100 long

100 long at 30° to horizontal

80 long at 60°
to horizontal

50 long

150 long at 15° to horizontal

Lines of inner polygon are all
parallel to and 30 inside outer
polygon

A Students AutoSketch   Chapter 6 Exercise 8

Fig. 6.23 Exercise 8

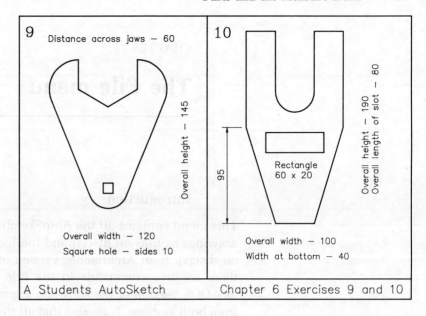

9   Distance across jaws — 60

Overall height — 145

Overall width — 120
Sqaure hole — sides 10

A Students AutoSketch

10

Overall height — 190
Overall length of slot — 80

95

Rectangle
60 x 20

Overall width — 100
Width at bottom — 40

Chapter 6 Exercises 9 and 10

Fig. 6.24 Exercises 9 and 10

CHAPTER 7

The File menu

Introduction

This menu contains all the AutoSketch commands for the saving of
drawings as files on disc(s) and the loading of drawings from files
on disc(s). If an Archimedes version of AutoSketch is being used,
there are two commands in the File menu not included in the
MS–DOS version of the software. Figure 7.1 shows the File menus
from both systems. Note also that all the Archimedes menus appear
on screen in a different style of text from that in which the
MS–DOS menus appear.

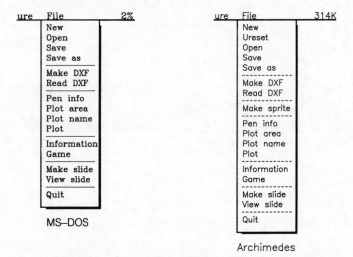

Fig. 7.1 The AutoSketch File
pull-down menu in both
MS–DOS and Archimedes
systems

Note: When typing filenames into the various dialogue boxes
associated with the items in the File menu, do not include the
MS–DOS drawing extensions *.dwg*, *.dxf*, *.sld*, or *.plt* with the
filenames or the sub-directory names *SKD*, *DXF*, *SLD*, *PLT* or
SPRITE when using the Archimedes version of AutoSketch.

There are six groups of menu items (commands) in the MS–DOS
version File menu – seven in the case of the Archimedes version:

1. four for opening and saving of AutoSketch drawing files (*SKD* files);
2. two for making and reading of Data Exchange Files (*DXF* files);
3. four for printing or plotting drawings;
4. two items, one of which brings information about the AutoSketch software currently being used onto the screen, the second brings a game to the screen;
5. two for making and viewing of Slide files (SLD files);
6. a command to quit from AutoSketch;
7. in the Archimedes version two extra menu items, Ureset and Make sprite, will be found.

Opening and saving files

The menu item New

When **New** is selected from the **File** menu:

1. if a new drawing has been constructed and saved as a file onto disc, the screen clears;
2. if a new drawing has been constructed and not saved to disc the warning dialogue box shown in Fig. 7.2 appears on screen;
3. if a drawing has been loaded from disc onto the screen and no alterations or additions have been made, the screen clears. The

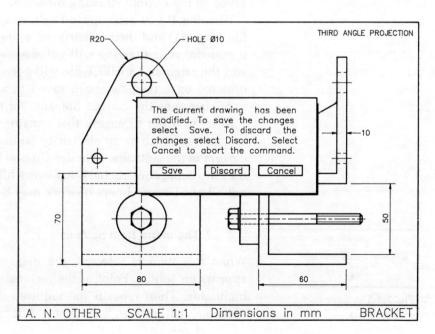

The current drawing has been modified. To save the changes select Save. To discard the changes select Discard. Select Cancel to abort the command.

Save   Discard   Cancel

Fig. 7.2 The warning dialogue box appearing when Save is attempted after additions made to a drawing

smallest of additions or amendments will cause the warning box (Fig. 7.2) to appear.

The Archimedes menu item Ureset

This menu item enables the operator to change the disc drive to and from which files are saved and opened. If this command is used there is no need to type in the disc drive letter in the dialogue boxes associated with opening and saving files. This item is not available on the MS–DOS version of the software.

The menu item Open

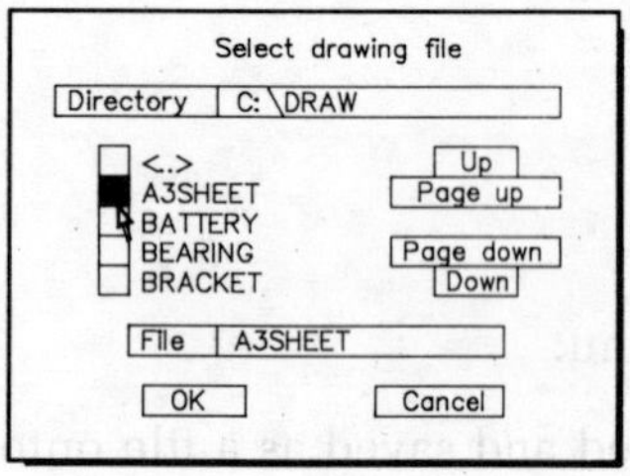

Select **Open** from the **File** menu and a dialogue box such as shown in Fig. 7.3 appears on screen. Selection of the required drawing file name by pointing, followed by selecting OK, brings that drawing on screen.

Note that the **Select drawing file** dialogue box of the Archimedes version of AutoSketch can show up to twelve files or directories as against the five possible with the MS–DOS version.

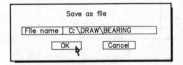

Fig. 7.3 The Open dialogue box

The menu item Save

When this item is selected the drawing on screen is automatically saved to the current drawing filename.

Warning: if you have opened a drawing file such as the A3SHEET file (page 31) and then constructed a drawing, do not select Save – if you do, your drawing will automatically be saved as A3SHEET and the original A3SHEET file will become a backup file. Once the drawing on screen has been saved to another filename, that filename becomes the current filename for the drawing.

Note: in order to ensure that constructions are not lost through breakdowns such as an electricity failure or some other accidental closure of the software, save drawings at regular intervals of time as they are being constructed – say every fifteen minutes. If this rule is not adopted many hours of work may be lost accidentally.

The menu item Save as

When this item is selected, the dialogue box shown in Fig. 7.4 appears on screen. Point at the rectangle **File name**. The rectangle highlights. Then type in the required drawing file directory and filename (without an extension). After checking that the correct

Fig. 7.4 The Save as dialogue box

name and directory have been typed in, select OK and the drawing will be saved to disc.

Note: AutoSketch drawing files in MS–DOS will have a filename extension of *.skd*. Drawing files in Archimedes are saved in a sub-directory *SKD*. A drawing with a filename of *part01* in MS–DOS will be saved as *part01.skd*. The same drawing in Archimedes would be saved as *SKD.PART01*. Either lower case or capital letters can be used in both systems.

DXF files

Data Exchange Files (DXF files) enable AutoSketch drawings to be read into other CAD (Computer Aided Drawing) software packages which have a DXF facility. For example – AutoSketch DXF files can be read into AutoCAD. Similarly AutoCAD 2D drawings can be read into AutoSketch. Some parts of some AutoCAD 2D drawings will not read into AutoSketch – an example being section hatching, which in AutoCAD is drawn as a block. Layers between AutoCAD and AutoSketch will have different names, but this does not cause much difficulty in practice.

Note: DXF files in MS–DOS have filenames such as *part01.dxf*. In Archimedes such files will be in a sub-directory *DXF*, with a full filename of *dxf.part01*.

The menu item Make DXF

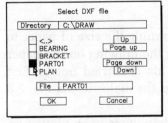

Fig. 7.5 The Write DXF dialogue box

To save a drawing as a DXF file select this menu item. A dialogue box such as shown in Fig. 7.5 appears on screen. Point at the **File name** rectangle and type in the required filename (without its *.dxf* extension). Then select OK and the drawing will be saved to disc as a DXF file.

The menu item Read DXF

To open a DXF file (whether from AutoSketch or another CAD system) select **Read DXF**. A dialogue box such as Fig. 7.6 appears on screen. Select the required filename, followed by pointing at **OK** and the drawing will appear on screen.

Fig. 7.6 The Read DXF dialogue box

Printing and plotting

Menu item Pen info

When **Pen info** is selected a dialogue box such as that shown in Fig. 7.7 appears. The exact style of the dialogue box will depend upon the plotter attached to the computer. If wishing to plot in a variety of colours, the pen numbers will need to be changed by pointing at the space below **Pen Number** and opposite the colour to be plotted by that pen. Colour pens would then be fitted into their numbered places in the plotter prior to plotting. When a drawing is to be plotted with two thicknesses of black lines – common practice in engineering and building drawings – a procedure such as the following would be suitable:

1. all outlines to be plotted in say 0.6 mm thickness drawn as black lines;
2. all other lines such as hidden detail, centre lines, dimension lines, etc., to be plotted as, say, 0.3 mm thickness drawn as red lines;
3. a black 0.6 mm pen is fitted as Pen Number 1 in the plotter;
4. a black 0.3 mm pen is fitted as Pen Number 2 in the plotter;
5. in the dialogue box **Black** is allocated **Pen Number 1** and **Red** allocated **Pen Number 2**;
6. **Pen Speed** is left as **5** – or slower if desired.

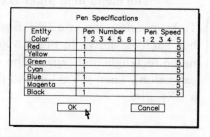

Fig. 7.7 The Pen info
dialogue box

Menu item Plot area

Before plotting can proceed details concerning the size of paper to be used for the plot, and the position of the drawing on the paper when it is plotted, must be decided. This is carried out by first selecting the **Plot area** item, which brings the dialogue box Fig. 7.8 on screen.

In the example shown in Fig. 7.8 the drawing is to be plotted on an A4 sheet, the sizes of which are in millimetres. As the original

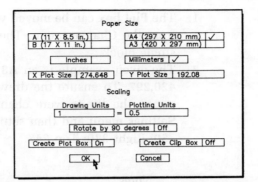

Fig. 7.8 The Plot area
dialogue box

drawing was drawn on an A3SHEET drawing, it must be plotted
half scale, so the **Plotting Units** are 0.5 of the **Drawing Units**. This
could also have been given as **Drawing Units** 2 times the **Plotting
Units**. The drawing does not require to be rotated through 90
degrees, so that item is left. **Create Clip Box** is left as **Off**.

It is advisable to show the **Plot box** around a drawing before it is
plotted. Figure 7.9 shows how a plot box will appear around a
drawing when the **Create Plot Box** detail is **On**. In this example, the
drawing had to be zoomed to a scale of **0.5** before the plot box
could be seen. It is almost inevitable that the position of the **Plot
box** will have to be changed to allow correct positioning of the
drawing on the paper when plotting takes place. This can be
achieved by using either of the two following methods.

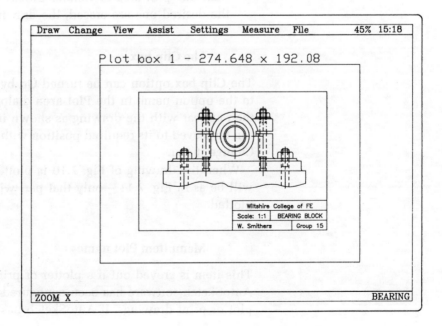

Fig. 7.9 A plot box around a
drawing

1. The **Plot box** can be moved with the aid of the **Move** command from the **Change** menu. The **Plot box** and its title move as a single block.
2. The given example is an A3 drawing made with **Limits** set to 420,297. To ensure the drawing will plot in the centre of the paper, the limits were changed by selecting **Limits** from the **Settings** menu and then setting the limits to: Left –50; Bottom –50; Right 370; Top 247.

Notes

1. Of these two options, the first is the easier.
2. The position of the drawing within its Plot box is saved with the drawing file on disc.
3. If a printer is connected to the computer, the **Plot box** procedure is the same as when a plotter is in use. With a printer as the method of obtaining hard copy, it will normally be necessary for the Rotate by 90 degrees option to be On.
4. If the **Plot box** appearing with the drawing is not satisfactory, it can be re-arranged by calling back the **Plot area** dialogue box and amending its details, e.g., the **Plotting** or **Drawing Units**. A second **Plot box** will then appear with the drawing (Plot box 2). However if more than one **Plot box** is left with the drawing before plotting, a warning box will appear stating that more than one plot area is visible. Unless all Plot boxes other than the desired one are erased, the drawing will not plot.

The Clip box

The **Clip box** option can be turned **On** by pointing at the box next to the option name in the **Plot area** dialogue box. A **Clip box** will then appear with the drawing as shown in Fig. 7.10. The **Clip box** can be moved to its required position with the aid of **Move** from the **Change** menu.

When the drawing of Fig. 7.10 is plotted (or printed), the result will be as in Fig. 7.11 – only that part within the Clip box will be plotted.

Menu item Plot name

This item is greyed out if a plotter or printer is connected and the AutoSketch software has been configured when first set up only to plot or print drawings. If AutoSketch has been configured to write

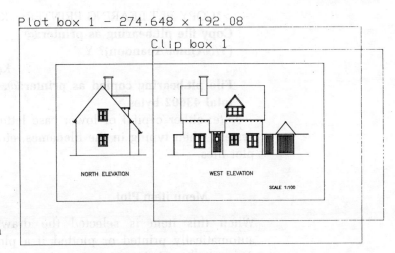

Fig. 7.10 A Clip box moved to a position to clip part of a drawing when plotting

Fig. 7.11 The result of plotting with a Clip box in position

Fig. 7.12 The Plot name dialogue box

drawings to a plot file, then this menu item will not be greyed out. If a drawing is to be saved as a plot file:

1. determine the **Plot area** box with the aid of the menu item **Plot area**;
2. select **Plot name**. The dialogue box Fig. 7.12 appears. Point at the **File name** rectangle and type in the required filename, not forgetting the drive, directory and sub-directory names if needed. Do not include the extension *.plt* (MS–DOS) or the sub-directory *PLT* (Archimedes);
3. select menu item **Plot**. The drawing will be saved to a plot file with the extension *.plt* (MS–DOS) or in the *PLT* sub-directory (Archimedes).

Plot files are saved in the form:

1. in an MS–DOS environment the drawing will be saved as a file with the extension *.plt*;
2. in an Archimedes environment the drawing will be saved in a sub-directory *PLT*.

The advantage of saving a drawing as a plot file is that it can then be printed without the aid of the AutoSketch software, but direct from the computer. To print a plot file:

1. MS–DOS – from the C:\> prompt (or it might be from A:\> or B:\> depending on which disc the plot file is held):
    C:\>COPY DRAW\BEARING.PLT PRN:

    Keyboard   Return

    and the drawing will print.
2. Archimedes from the > prompt:

>*COPY PLT.BEARING PRINTER: *Keyboard   Return*
Copy file plt.bearing as printer:@
(Y/N/Quiet/Abandon)? Y

Keyboard   Return
File plt.bearing copied as printer:@, 43 Kbytes 1 file copied,
total 43602 bytes

Note: either capital or lower case letters can be used in either system when typing in the filenames, etc, for printing or plotting plot files.

Menu item Plot

When this item is selected the drawing on screen will be automatically printed or plotted if a plot box has already been determined and the printer or plotter is connected and switched on. If a **Plot box** has not already been determined the dialogue box Fig. 7.13 appears for determining the details of the **Plot box** and **Clip box** (if used). The disadvantage of not determining the **Plot box** prior to plotting is that the operator has no real control over the positioning of the drawing on the sheet. This may not matter if **Limits** have previously been set for positioning drawings when plotted. Note Fig. 7.13 is almost identical to Fig. 7.8.

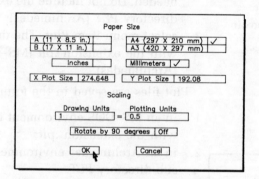

Fig. 7.13 The Plot dialogue box

Information and Game

Menu item Information

When **Information** is selected, details of the software and its version number of the software appears on screen.

Menu item Game

Selecting **Game** makes a noughts-and-crosses game appear. Bored operators can while away a few minutes trying to beat the machine at playing the game. I find this game to be an excellent test of man against machine.

Slide files

Slide files can be used in either AutoSketch or AutoCAD. AutoSketch Slide files are in fact in AutoCAD format. They are useful files for storing drawings in a form which does not use as much disc space as drawing files and they can be recalled to screen very quickly. Slide file drawings cannot be saved as drawing files or plotted. They are only intended for display purposes. For example they allow one to browse quickly through sets of drawings or they can be used in visual demonstrations by computer to audiences.

Slide files are saved in MS–DOS with the extension *.sld* and in Archimedes in a sub-directory *SLD*.

Menu item Make slide

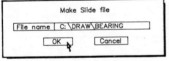

Fig. 7.14 The Make slide dialogue box

When a drawing is to be saved as a slide file, select this item from the **File** menu and type in the required filename in the box provided in the dialogue box which appears on screen – Fig. 7.14. Do not include MS–DOS extension .sld or Archimedes SLD sub-directory name. Then select OK and the drawing is saved as a slide file.

Menu item View slide

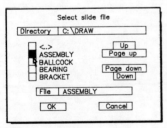

Fig. 7.15 The View slide dialogue box

When wishing to bring a Slide file on screen, select the **View Slide** item. A dialogue box appears – Fig. 7.15 – from which the required file can be selected. The drawing then appears on screen – very quickly.

Menu item Quit

Select this item when the session of using the software has finished. If unsaved items are on screen the warning Fig. 7.2 appears. If no extra details have been added to the drawing on screen since it was last opened or saved, the computer takes the operator out of AutoSketch.

The Archimedes menu item Make sprite

A drawing on screen can be saved as an Archimedes sprite with the aid of this item. Such sprite drawings, held in a sub-directory SPRITE, can be included as drawing from AutoSketch when some word processor or desk editing programmes are being used. Sprites can also be called on screen outside AutoSketch, by first loading the sprite in the following manner:

*SLOAD SKETCH.SPRITE.BEARING *Keyboard Return*

followed by:

*RUN SKETCH.SPRITE.BEARING *Keyboard Return*

and the sprite drawing appears on screen.

Note: The Sprite menu item is only available in the Archimedes version of AutoSketch.

CHAPTER 8

Step-by-step construction of AutoSketch drawings

Layers

Drawings in AutoSketch can be constructed on a number of **Layers**. When a drawing is constructed on layers, it is as if it had been drawn on a series of tracing films of absolute transparency, each fitting perfectly over the other tracings in the drawing. In AutoSketch, if the layer containing part of a construction is in position, it is said to be **Visible**. If not in position it is said to be invisible. The state of layers – whether visible or not – is shown by ticks (visible) when the **Layer** item is selected from the **Settings** menu. The resulting dialogue box is shown in Fig. 8.1, in which it can be seen that all layers are visible. To make a layer invisible, point at the rectangle beside the layer number and press the pointing device button. The tick will disappear and the layer becomes invisible.

The drawing of a bracket in Fig. 8.1 was constructed on seven

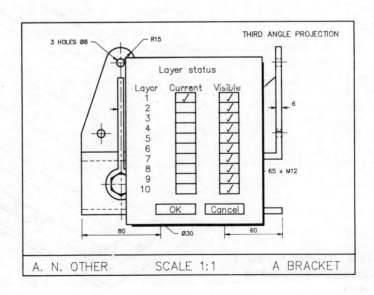

Fig. 8.1 The Layer dialogue box

layers. These are shown in diagrammatic form in Fig. 8.2. The use of layers when drawing in AutoSketch has several advantages.

1. Each type of detail on its own layer can have its own colour and line type. The colour allows the type of detail to show clearly on screen.
2. If a drawing becomes crowded with detail, layers not in use can be made invisible, thus clearing some of the detail from the screen and making for easier construction.
3. When layers not being worked on are made invisible, **Redraws** and the regeneration of the screen after zooms becomes much quicker. This can speed up work considerably, particularly when working on complex drawings.

The methods of constructing two drawings with the aid of AutoSketch are described in a step-by-step procedure in this chapter. The menus, menu items, prompts and action to be taken to produce the constructions follow the same form as in earlier chapters:

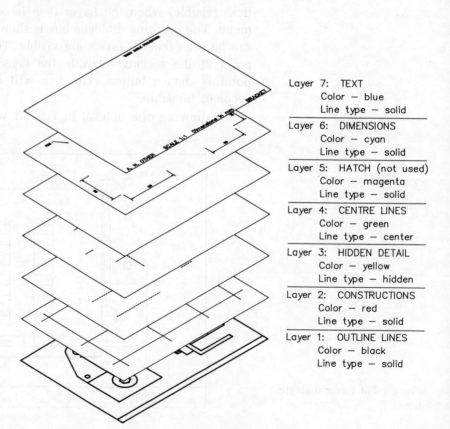

Layer 7: TEXT
          Color – blue
          Line type – solid

Layer 6: DIMENSIONS
          Color – cyan
          Line type – solid

Layer 5: HATCH (not used)
          Color – magenta
          Line type – solid

Layer 4: CENTRE LINES
          Color – green
          Line type – center

Layer 3: HIDDEN DETAIL
          Color – yellow
          Line type – hidden

Layer 2: CONSTRUCTIONS
          Color – red
          Line type – solid

Layer 1: OUTLINE LINES
          Color – black
          Line type – solid

Fig. 8.2 Theoretical view of a drawing constructed on Layers

Menu	Item	Action
1. **File**	**Open**	Dialogue box settings:
		Select drawing file A3SHEET
		point
2. **Draw**	**Line**	add construction lines

A3SHEET is the name of the file on which the drawings are constructed in both examples.

First example – an engineering drawing

This drawing is to be constructed on the following layers:

Layer 1 – Outlines	– Solid line, Black;
Layer 2 – Constructions	– Solid line, Red;
Layer 3 – Hidden detail	– Hidden line, Yellow;
Layer 4 – Centre lines	– Center line, Green;
Layer 5 – Hatch lines	– Solid line, Magenta;
Layer 6 – Dimensions	– Solid line, Cyan;
Layer 7 – Text	– Solid line, Blue.

Notes

1. In AutoSketch, before any detail of a construction can be added to a drawing, the **Layer** number, the **Line type** and the **Color** to be used for the detail, must set each time a different form of detail is added to the drawing, e.g., for centre lines; for hidden detail lines; for text etc.
2. It is not absolutely necessary to construct a drawing on layers. Each different **Line type** and its **Color** can each be set on a single layer. The advantage of using layers is that they can be turned off when required. When a drawing become overcrowded with details, the ability to turn Layers off allows one to work on a screen which is less crowded. Because of this it is recommended that the habit of constructing drawings on layers is adopted.
3. Always **Save** a drawing under construction at regular intervals. Then, if anything goes wrong, e.g., power failure, an interruption, switching off the computer at a wrong moment; then at least that part of the construction drawn up to the last **Save** will be on file.
4. The procedures described below shown for constructing these two drawings appear as if they would take a considerable time.

It will be found that, after some practice with using the menus and menu items of AutoSketch, the time taken for constructing such drawings is far less than the time taken to read the descriptions.

Draw on the file A3SHEET:

Menu	Item	Action
1. **File**	**Open**	Dialogue box settings:
		Select drawing file A3SHEET *point*

Draw construction lines:

2. **Settings**	**Layer**	Dialogue box settings:
		Layer status 2 *point*
3. **Settings**	**Line type**	Dialogue box settings:
		Drawing Line Type Solid *point*
4. **Settings**	**Color**	Dialogue box settings:
		Drawing Color Red *point*
5. **Draw**	**Line**	draw construction lines (Fig. 8.3)

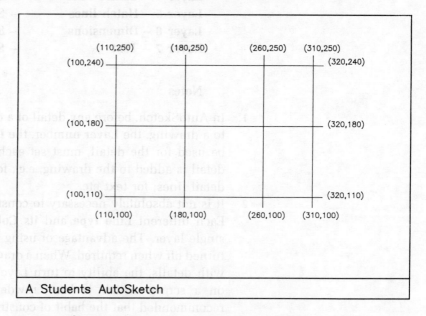

Fig. 8.3 Constructing an engineering drawing – Stage 1

Draw outlines:

6. **Settings**	**Layer**	Dialogue box settings
		Layer status 1 *point*
7. **Settings**	**Line type**	Dialogue box settings
		Drawing Line Type Solid *point*
8. **Settings**	**Color**	Dialogue box settings
		Drawing Color Black *point*
9. **Draw**	**Polygon**	outlines as numbered (Fig. 8.4)

10. **Draw**	**Line**	add lines to end view (Fig. 8.4)
11. **Draw**	**Polygon**	draw front view of web (Fig. 8.4)
12. **File**	**Save as**	Dialogue box settings
		Save as file HANGER *Keyboard*

Note: the file name (bottom right on prompt line) changes to HANGER.

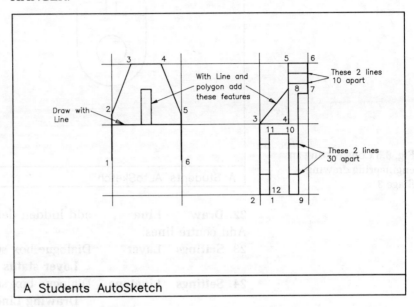

Fig. 8.4 Constructing an engineering drawing – Stage 2

13. **Draw**	**Arc**	arc on front view (Fig. 8.5)
14. **Draw**	**Circle**	circles on front view (Fig. 8.5)
15. **Settings**	**Fillet**	Dialogue box settings
		Fillet radius 10 *Keyboard OK*
16. **Change**	**Fillet**	

17. **Fillet Select line(s):** Select (Fig. 8.5)
　　dialogue box appears – **polygon has been selected**
　　　　　　　　　　　Dialogue box settings
　　　　　　　　　　　　　　　Yes *point*
　　　　　　　　　　　point to fillet lines

Make construction layer 2 invisible:

18. **Settings**	**Layer**	Dialogue box settings
		Layer status 2 (Visible) *point*

Add hidden detail:

19. **Settings**	**Layer**	Dialogue box settings
		Layer status 3 *point*
20. **Settings**	**Color**	Dialogue box settings
		Drawing Color Yellow *point*
21. **Settings**	**Line type**	Dialogue box settings
		Drawing Line Type Hidden *point*

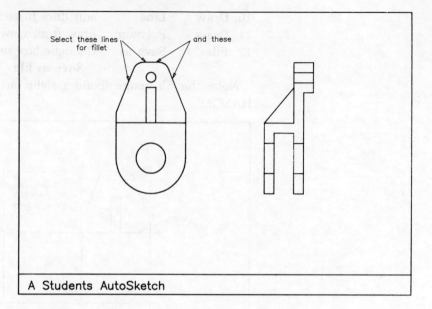

Fig. 8.5 Constructing an
engineering drawing –
Stage 3

22. **Draw   Line**   add hidden detail (Fig. 8.6)
Add centre lines:
23. **Settings   Layer**   Dialogue box settings
                            Layer status 4 *point*
24. **Settings   Linetype**   Dialogue box settings
                            Drawing Line Type Center *point*
25. **Settings   Color**   Dialogue box settings
                            Drawing Color Green *point*

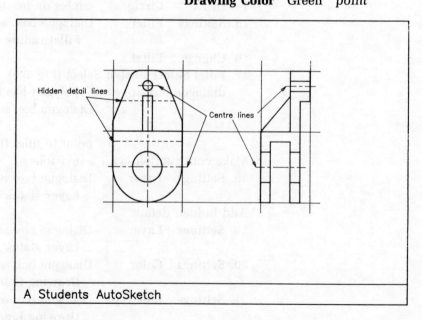

Fig. 8.6 Constructing an
engineering drawing –
Stage 4

26. **Draw**   **Line**   add centre lines (Fig. 8.6)

Add hatching:

27. **Settings** **Layer**   Dialogue box settings
                                    Layer status   5   *point*
28. **Settings** **Linetype**   Dialogue box settings
                                    Drawing Line Type Solid   *point*
29. **Settings** **Color**   Dialogue box settings
                                    Drawing Color Magenta *point*
30. **Draw**   **Line**   draw start line (Fig. 8.7)
31. **Settings** **Box Array**   Dialogue box settings

Row distance	4	*Keyboard*	*OK*
Column distance	0	*Keyboard*	*OK*
Rows	25	*Keyboard*	*OK*
Columns	1	*Keyboard*	*OK*
Baseline angle	0	*Keyboard*	*OK*

32. **Change**   **Box Array**
    Prompt   *Action*

Box Array Select object: select the line drawn   *point*
                              with **Box Array Settings** and **Box Array**
                              hatch (Fig. 8.7)

Repeat 26 to 32 for remainder of hatching

33. **File**   **Save**   None, drawing automatically saved as
                                    HANGER.SKD

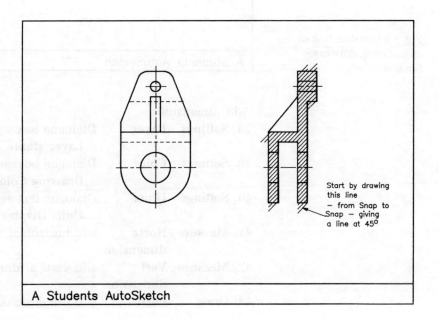

Fig. 8.7 Constructing an
engineering drawing –
Stage 5

Start by drawing
this line
– from Snap to
Snap – giving
a line at 45°

A Students AutoSketch

34. **Change**	**Erase**	
Prompt		Action
Erase Select object:		Select hatch lines to be completely erased
35. **Change**	**Break**	
Prompt		Action
Break Select object:		select in turn each object to be broken until the hatch pattern is completed (Fig. 8.8)
36. **View**	**Zoom box**	to obtain the necessary degree of accuracy for breaking lines in the hatch pattern
37. **File**	**Save**	button

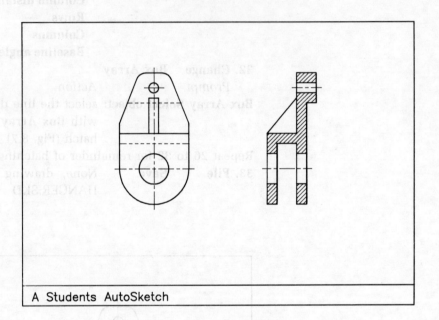

A Students AutoSketch

Fig. 8.8 Constructing an engineering drawing – Stage 6

Add dimensions:

38. **Settings**	**Layer**	Dialogue box settings
		Layer status 6 *point*
39. **Settings**	**Color**	Dialogue box settings
		Drawing Color Cyan *point*
40. **Settings**	**Units**	Dialogue box settings
		Units Display Format **0 digits**
41. **Measure**	**Horiz dimension**	add horizontal dimensions (Fig. 8.9)
42. **Measure**	**Vert dimension**	add vertical dimensions (Fig. 8.9)
43. **Draw**	**Parts**	add dimensions not horiz or vert

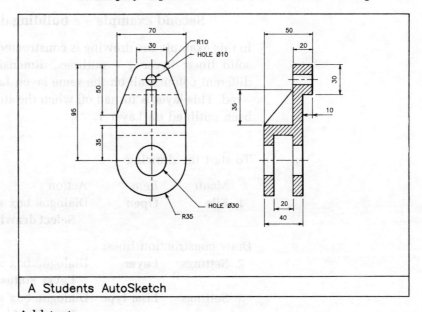

Fig. 8.9 Constructing an
engineering drawing –
Stage 7

Add text:

44. Settings	**Layer**	Dialogue box settings
		Layer status 7 *point*
45. Settings	**Color**	Dialogue box settings
		Drawing Color Blue *point*
46. Draw	**Text**	add text (Fig. 8.10)
47. Settings	**Text**	Dialogue box settings
		Height 8 *Keyboard OK*
		Add HANGER BRACKET (Fig. 8.10)
48. File	**Save**	*button*

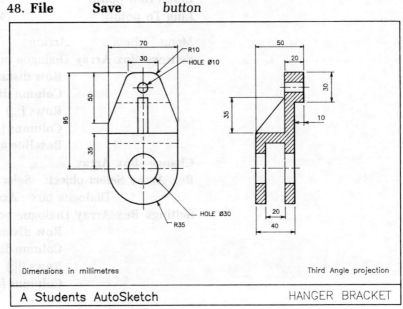

Fig. 8.10 Constructing an
engineering drawing –
Stage 8

Second example – a building drawing

In this example the drawing is constructed on two layers using only
solid lines; Layer 1 – outlines, dimensions and text, each with
different colours, all on the same layer; Layer 2 – construction grid
– red. This layer is turned off when the structure of the drawing has
been outlined on Layer 1.

To start the drawing:

	Menu	Item	Action
	Menu	*Item*	*Action*
1.	**File**	**Open**	Dialogue box settings:
			Select drawing file A3SHEET *point*

Draw construction lines:

	Menu	Item	Action
2.	**Settings**	**Layer**	Dialogue box settings:
			Layer status 2 *point*
3.	**Settings**	**Line type**	Dialogue box settings:
			Drawing Line Type Solid *point*
4.	**Settings**	**Color**	Dialogue box settings:
			Drawing Color Red *point*
5.	**Draw**	**Line**	draw construction grid (Fig. 8.11)

The construction grid is drawn as follows:

Prompt	Action
Prompt	*Action*
Line From point:	60,270 *Keyboard Return*
Line To point:	60,10 *Keyboard Return*
Line From point:	40,270 *Keyboard Return*
Line To point:	460,270 *Keyboard Return*

Menu	Item	Action		
Menu	*Item*	*Action*		
Settings	**Box Array**	Dialogue box settings		
		Row distance	0	*Keyboard OK*
		Column distance	20	*Keyboard OK*
		Rows (‖‖)	1	*Keyboard OK*
		Columns (---)	20	*Keyboard OK*
		Baseline angle	0	*Keyboard OK*
Change	**Box Array**			
Box Array Select object: Select vertical line				
		Dialogue box **Accept Modify** Accept *point*		
Settings	**Box Array**	Dialogue box settings		
		Row distance	−20	*Keyboard OK*
		Column distance	0	*Keyboard OK*
		Rows (‖‖)	20	*Keyboard OK*
		Columns (---)	0	*Keyboard OK*

Change Box Array
Box Array Select object: Select horizontal line
                          Dialogue box   **Accept Modify**   Accept *point*

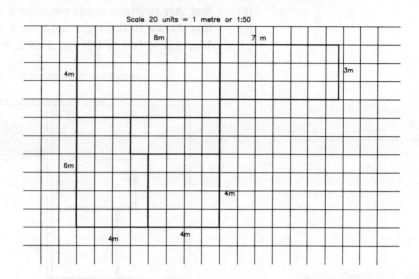

Scale 20 units = 1 metre or 1:50

Fig. 8.11 Constructing a
building drawing – Stage 1

Construct structure of plan:

Menu	Item	Action			
6. **Settings**	**Layer**	Dialogue box settings			
		Layer status 1 *point*			
7. **Settings**	**Color**	Dialogue box settings			
		Drawing Color Black *point*			
8. **Draw**	**Polygon**	draw outline (Fig. 8.11)			
9. **File**	**Save as**	Dialogue box settings			
		Save as file BUILDING *Keyboard* OK			

Add wall and partition thicknesses (Fig. 12):

10. **Settings**	**Box Array**	Dialogue box settings			
		Row distance	5	*Keyboard*	OK
		Column distance	0	*Keyboard*	OK
		Rows (‖)	2	*Keyboard*	OK
		Columns (---)	1	*Keyboard*	OK
		Baseline angle	0	*Keyboard*	OK
11. **Change**	**Box Array**				

Prompt	*Action*
Box Array Select object:	Select horizontal lines to produce the outer wall thicknesses;

then set the **Box Array** settings to either 5,–5, 2 or–2 in Row or

Column distances to complete the drawing Fig. 8.12. Remember that:

(a) a **Box Array** upwards requires a +ve Row number;

(b) a **Box Array** downwards requires a −ve Row number;

(c) a **Box Array** to the right requires a +ve Column number;

(d) a **Box Array** to the left requires a −ve Column number;

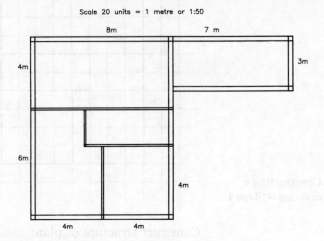

Scale 20 units = 1 metre or 1:50

Fig. 8.12 Constructing a
building drawing – Stage 2

To complete the walls and partitions (Fig. 8.13):

12. **Change   Break**

Prompt	Action
Break Select object:	point
Break First point:	point
Break Second point:	point

and so on to break all lines crossing wall and partition joins as in Fig. 8.13. Menu **View**, item **Zoom box** will be needed where partition lines meet partition and/or wall lines. It should be possible to **Break** wall to wall joins with ease because in the A3 sheet file, **Snap** is set to 5 (the same as the wall thicknesses).

Add doors and windows (Fig. 8.14):

Doors and windows can be added as **Parts** (see pages 70–87). If suitable door and window drawing files are already on disc, these can be added to the drawing as **Parts**. If such files are not on disc, construct the necessary door and window drawing files, save each one in turn and load them in position on the drawing as **Parts** as required then **Break** those lines of wall and partitions which are no longer necessary (Fig. 8.14).

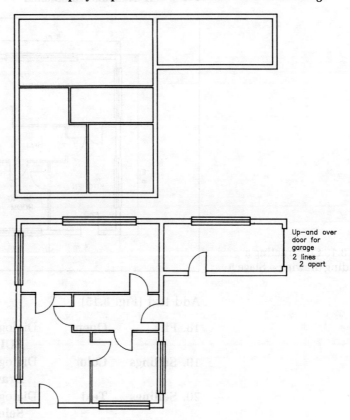

Fig. 8.13 Constructing a
building drawing – Stage 3

Fig. 8.14 Constructing a
building drawing – Stage 4

Add Up-and-over door to garage – see Fig. 8.14:

13. **File**   **Save**   *button*

Add dimensions (Fig. 8.15):

14. **File**   **Open**   Dialogue box settings
                                 A3SHEET   *point*

15. **Draw**   **Line**

Prompt	Action
Line From point:	100,100 *Keyboard* *Return*
Line To point:	P(14,315) *Keyboard* *Return*

16. **Settings**   **Part base**   Dialogue box settings
                                 Set by pointing   *point*
                                 Point at centre of line just drawn

17. **File**   **Save as**   Dialogue box settings
                                 File name   ARROW   *OK*

The file – ARROW – can now be repeatedly called as a **Part** to be
inserted at the ends of lines drawn to dimension the outer wall of
the building plan (colour cyan). The dimension figures are added
as text (colour cyan, height 5).

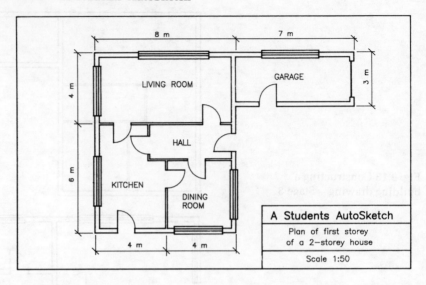

Fig. 8.15 Constructing a
building drawing – Stage 5

Add text (Fig. 8.15)

18. **File**	**Open**	Dialogue box settings
		BUILDING point
19. **Settings**	**Color**	Dialogue box settings
		Drawing Color Cyan point
20. **Settings**	**Text**	Dialogue box settings
		Select Font to Load ROMANS point
		Load Font point
		Pick Active Font ROMANS point
		Height 6 Keyboard OK
21. **Draw**	**Text**	

Prompt	Action
Text Enter point:	add text LIVING ROOM, GARAGE, HALL, KITCHEN, DINING ROOM; Plan of first storey of a 2-storey house; Scale 1:50
	Keyboard Return after each line of text.

Menu	Item	Action
22. **Settings**	**Text**	Dialogue box settings
		Height 8 Keyboard OK
23. **Settings**	**Color**	Dialogue box settings
		Drawing Color Black point
24. **Draw**	**Text**	
	Text Enter point:	Add text – A Students AutoSketch
		Keyboard Return

| 25. **Draw** | **Line** | add border and title box lines |
| 26. **File** | **Save as** | Dialogue box settings |

File name BUILDING *Keyboard*   OK

CHAPTER 9

Pictorial drawing and hatching

Pictorial drawing

AutoSketch is a CAD software package for constructing two-dimensional (2D) drawings and has no three-dimensional (3D) facilities. Pictorial drawings such as isometric drawings are not true 3D drawings. AutoSketch does not have commands for drawing in isometric, or in any other type of pictorial drawing. Despite this various forms of pictorial drawings can be constructed in AutoSketch. In this chapter, methods of constructing pictorial drawings in isometric, oblique, planometric and estimated perspective are described.

Isometric drawing

The grid of dots produced on screen when **Grid** is **On** cannot be set other than in vertical and horizontal rows. However the **Y Spacing** of the grid can be different from **X Spacing**. This also applies to the setting of **Snap**. By taking advantage of these differences, **Grid** and **Snap** can be set to assist in drawing reasonably accurate isometric drawings.

   With **Limits** set to give a screen suitable for constructing drawings for an A3 sheet, if both **Grid** and **Snap** are set to:

> **X Spacing** 10 (or a multiple of 10);
> **Y Spacing** 5.75 (or a multiple of 5.75);

then they are set so that when both are **On** they can be used to draw lines at 30° to horizontal to left and right and to 90° to horizontal. These **Grid** and **Snap** settings will actually produce lines at angles of 29.8989° – near enough to 30° for this form of pictorial drawing. If a precise 30° angle is thought to be necessary, set **Y Spacing** to 5.7735. This figure is, however, not so easy to handle when setting in multiples of 5.7735 as is 5.75.

Figure 9.1 is an example of a simple isometric drawing drawn on a grid, with **Grid** and **Snap X Spacings** of 20 and **Y Spacings** of 11.5 (twice the figures given above). When using such a grid, take care that the rubber band associated with drawing with the command **Line** (or **Polygon**) runs along the lines of grid dots when drawing at the 30° angles.

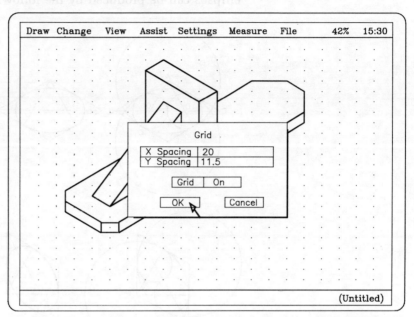

Fig. 9.1 A Grid suitable for isometric drawing

Figure 9.2 is another example of a simple isometric drawing drawn with straight lines on the recommended **Grid** and **Snap** settings.

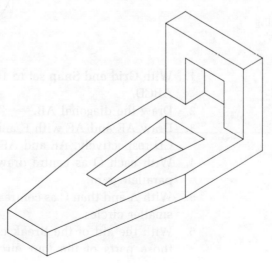

Fig. 9.2 An example of an isometric drawing constructed in AutoSketch

Drawing Isometric Circles

In isometric drawings, circles become ellipses. The ellipses will appear on the top surfaces, on the right-hand surfaces or on the left-hand surfaces of the isometric drawing. AutoSketch has no command system for producing ellipses. Approximate isometric ellipses can be produced by the following method, see Fig. 9.3.

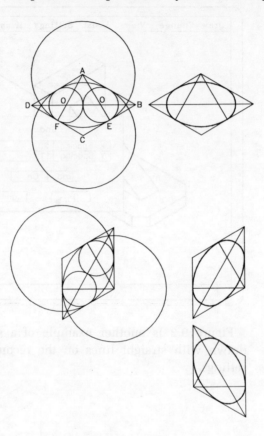

Fig. 9.3 Constructing
isometric 'ellipses'

1. With **Grid** and **Snap** set to 10 and 5.75, draw the parallelogram ABCD.
2. Draw the diagonal AB.
3. Draw AE and AF with E and F in the centres of lines BC and CD respectively. AE and AF meet AB at two points O.
4. With each O as centre draw circles touching the lines of the parallelogram.
5. With A and then C as centres, draw circles tangential to the two smaller circles.
6. With the aid of the **Break** command (**Change** menu) break off those parts of the four circles forming part of the isometric

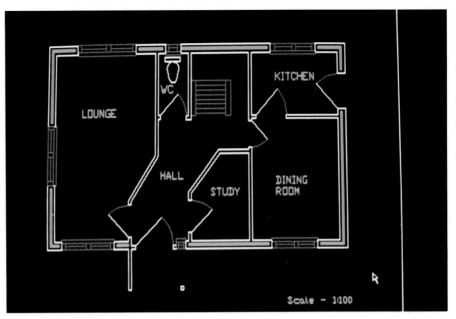

Plate I MS–DOS AutoSketch screen. Black background red text

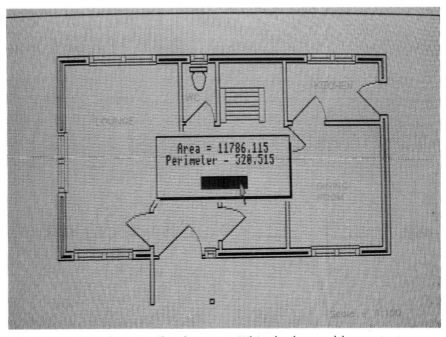

Plate II Archimedes AutoSketch screen. White background brown text

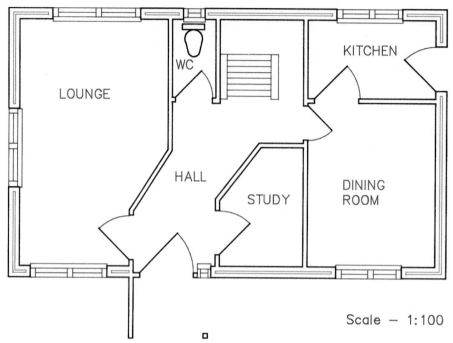

Plate III   A house plan plotted in four colours

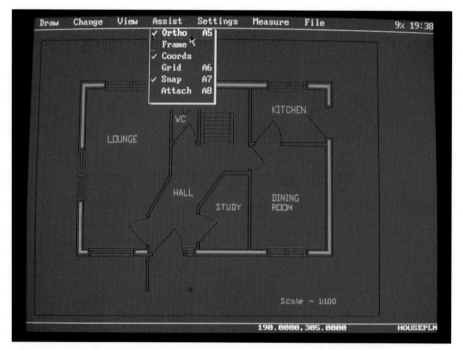

Plate IV   MS–DOS AutoSketch screen. Blue background white text

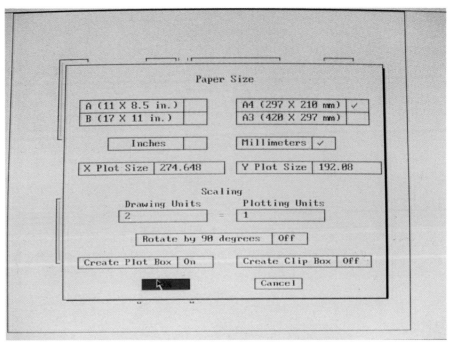

Plate V MS–DOS AutoSketch screen. Dialogue box for Plot area

NORTH ELEVATION   WEST ELEVATION

SCALE 1:100

Plate VI Building drawing elevations plotted in four colours

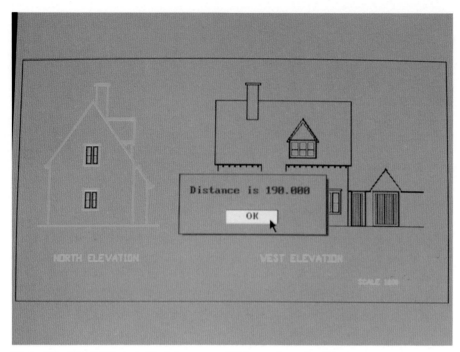

Plate VII MS–DOS AutoSketch screen. Dialogue box for Distance

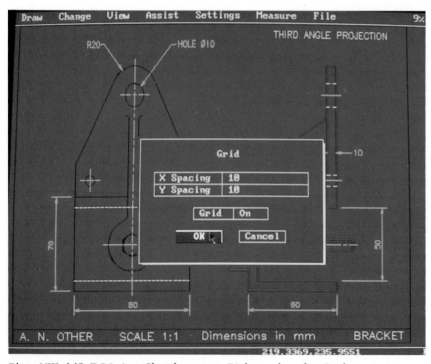

Plate VIII MS–DOS AutoSketch screen. Dialogue box for Grid

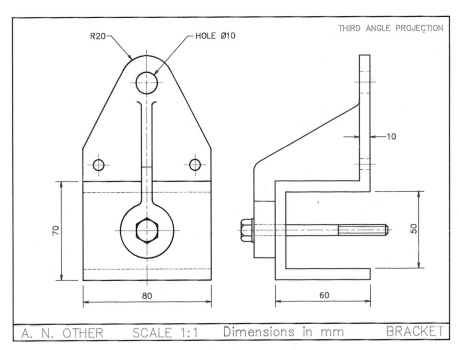

Plate IX An engineering drawing plotted in six colours

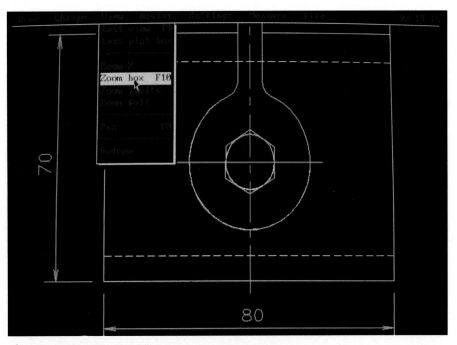

Plate X MS–DOS AutoSketch screen. View menu

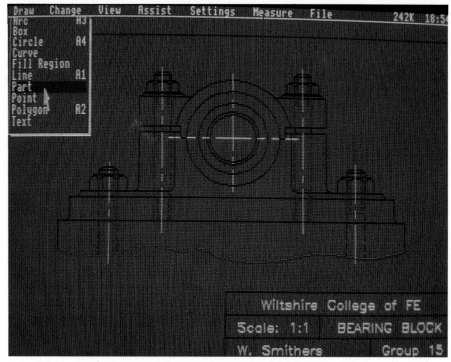

Plate XI   Archimedes AutoSketch screen. Draw menu

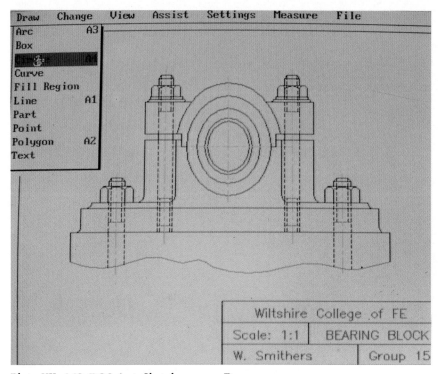

Plate XII   MS–DOS AutoSketch screen. Draw menu

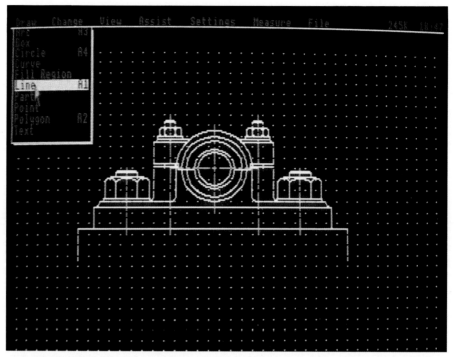

Plate XIII Archimedes AutoSketch screen. Screen with Grid dots

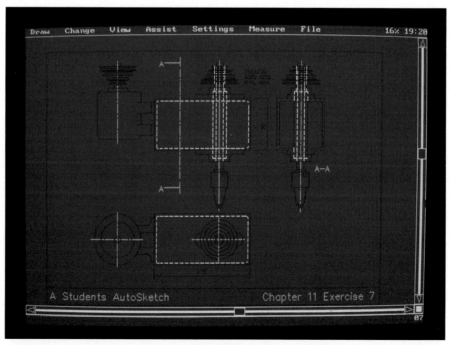

Plate XIV A Version 3 screen configured to show scrollbars

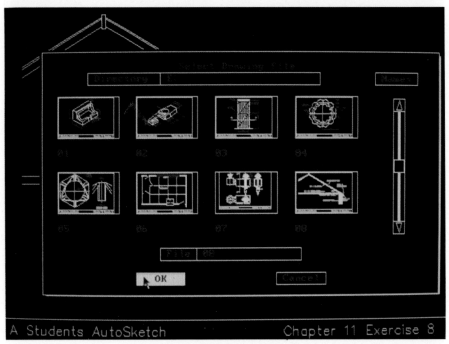

Plate XV   A Version 3 screen showing icons in a Select Drawing File dialogue box

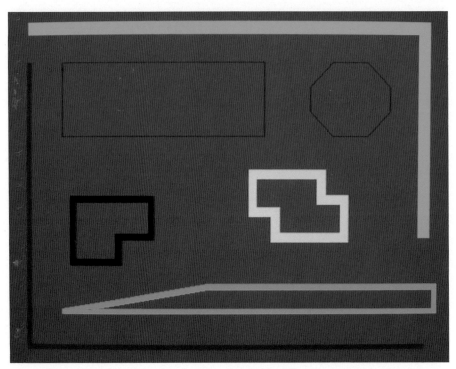

Plate XVI   A Version 3 screen showing Polylines of various widths and colours

'ellipse', this will give the top 'ellipse'.

7. Right-hand and left-hand 'ellipses' are constructed in a similar manner – lower drawings of Fig. 9.3. The left-hand 'ellipse' was formed by using the **Mirror** command on the right-hand 'ellipse'.

8. With **Erase** (**Change** menu) erase all straight lines from the three 'ellipses'. This leaves the three drawings shown in Fig. 9.4.

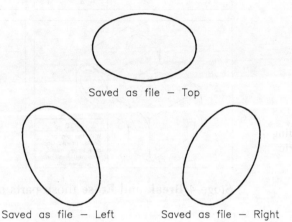

Saved as file – Top

Fig. 9.4 The three 'ellipses' for saving as Part files

Saved as file – Left   Saved as file – Right

Using these isometric 'ellipses' in drawings:

1. Save each ellipse with the file names as shown in Fig. 9.4, each with a **Part base** (see page 71). To do this, only one of the 'ellipses' should be on screen at any one Save.

2. When required for inclusion in a drawing, these files can be called as **Parts**.

3. With the aid of the menu items **Scale**, **Move**, **Copy** and **Break** (all in the **Change** menu), any size or part of an isometric 'ellipse' can be included in a pictorial drawing.

Figure 9.5 shows the stages by which the three isometric ellipses, saved as Part files, can be included as required in an isometric drawing:

Stage 1 draw the straight lines outline of the required drawing.
Stage 2 call the **Parts** files for the ellipses, placing them in any convenient position of the straight lines outline – they can be accurately positioned later.
Stage 3 with **Scale**, **Break**, **Copy** and **Move** alter the sizes and positions of the ellipses so that they are accurately placed on the drawing. Break those parts not needed.

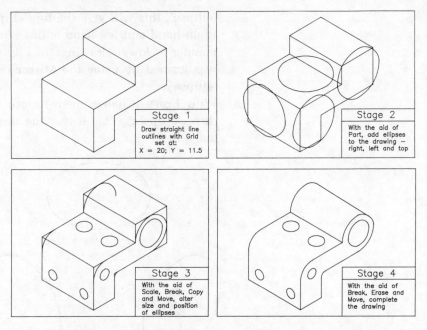

Fig. 9.5 Stages in adding ellipses to an isometric drawing

Stage 4 **Break** and **Erase** those parts of the drawing not required.

Notes:

1. When saving the Top, Right and Left ellipses as Part files, the four arcs forming each outline would have been **Group**ed in order to allow the Part to be moved or copied as one object. This means that when **Break**ing an ellipse within an isometric drawing it must first be **Ungroup**ed. This is done by using the command **Ungroup** (twice) from the **Change** menu.
2. When using **Scale** on a drawing, its size changes in 0.1 steps.

Isometric drawing using Polar coordinates

Isometric drawings can also be constructed using the Polar coordinate method of drawing lines at angles to the horizontal (page 21). For example with **Limits** set for A3 sheet size, one left-hand side of a drawing could be formed with the **Polygon** command from the **Draw** menu by:

Polygon From point: *point*
Polygon To point: p(100,150)   *Return*
Polygon To point: p(120,90)   *Return*
Polygon To point: p(100,330)   *Return*
Polygon To point: p(120,270)   *Return*

Other sides of the drawing could be constructed using the same method. If ellipses are to be added they could be added from the Part files as above. This method of drawing in isometric is not only rather time consuming, but requires care in ensuring that all numbers for coordinate points are accurately keyed.

Planometric drawing

With both **X Spacing** and **Y Spacing** set to the same figures for both **Grid** and **Snap**, 45°/45° planometric drawings can be constructed. This is because the diagonal across the **Grid** and **Snap** points will be at an angle of 45°. Figure 9.6 is an example of such a planometric drawing.

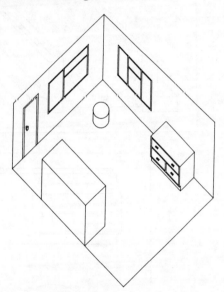

Fig. 9.6 An example of a simple 45°/45° planometric drawing

Oblique drawing

Oblique drawings can be constructed with receding sides drawn at an angle of 45° to the horizontal. Because of this feature, oblique drawings can be quickly constructed in AutoSketch, if both X and Y spacings for **Grid** and **Snap** are set to the same figures. Then lines drawn diagonally across the squares of the grid points will be at the required angle of 45°. Cabinet drawing – a type of oblique drawing, requires receding sides to be at 45°, with the lines at 45° being drawn to half the scale of the front faces of the drawing. Cabinet drawings can therefore also be drawn in AutoSketch. When drawing oblique or cabinet drawings with this software, it is advisable to ensure that all circles, circular arcs and curves of such drawings are in the front-facing planes. They can then be easily drawn with the **Circle**, **Arc** or **Curve** commands from the **Draw** menu. Examples of oblique drawings are given in Fig. 9.7. Examples of oblique cabinet drawings are given in Fig. 9.8.

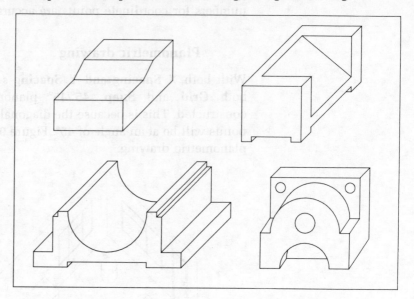

Fig. 9.7 Examples of oblique drawings constructed in AutoSketch

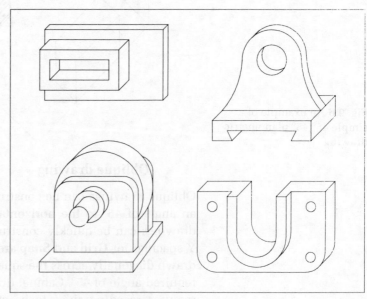

Fig. 9.8 Examples of cabinet drawings constructed in AutoSketch

Perspective drawing

True perspective drawing is not possible with AutoSketch. However estimated perspective drawing is possible. Figure 9.9 shows some examples. These were constructed as follows.

1. Select the positions of two vanishing points (VP1 and VP2) at estimated points on the screen. The two VPs must be horizontally in line with each other.
2. Construct by drawing lines from points on the drawing to the two VPs. Vertical lines are drawn vertically.
3. With the aid of the **Break** command, trim lines which stretch to the VPs from outside the required drawing.

Notes

1. To avoid distortion, select the two vanishing points and the position of the lowest corner of the drawing carefully.
2. Construction lines could be on layer 1 (red lines say), the final drawing on Layer 2 (black lines). Then turn layer 1 off, leaving only the final drawing on screen. This will avoid the use of **Break**.

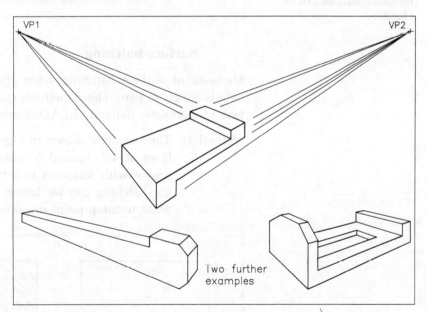

Fig. 9.9 Examples of simple estimated two-point perspective drawings constructed in AutoSketch

Summary

Figure 9.10 summarises the methods which can be used with AutoSketch for producing the four different types of pictorial drawings described above.

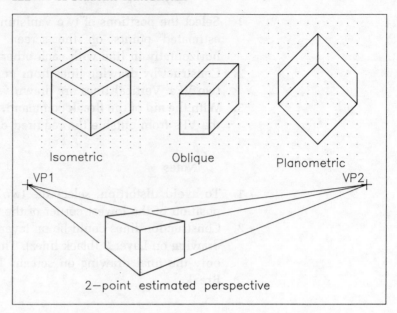

Fig. 9.10 A summary of the four pictorial drawing methods described in this chapter

Surface hatching

Methods of surface hatching were given on page 105. Further details are given here. These methods can be adopted to overcome a lack of automatic hatching in AutoSketch.

Method 1: The rectangle shown in Fig. 9.11 is to be hatched with lines at 45°, spaced 5 units apart. If the rectangle is drawn with **Snap** set to 5 units and On, the lines for the hatching can be drawn, one at a time, from **Snap** point to **Snap** point diagonally across the **Grid** points.

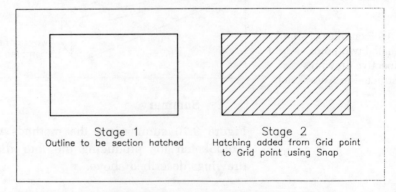

Fig. 9.11 Hatching from Snap to Snap points

Method 2: In Fig. 9.12 a second method is shown, one which makes use of the command **Box Array**.

Stage 1: draw a single line at 45°, from **Snap** to **Snap**;

Stage 2: with the aid of the command **Box Array** (page 52), copy the 45° line a requisite number of times to fill part of the area being hatched;

Stage 3: repeat for other parts which are to be hatched;

Stage 4: break those parts of the hatch lines that are not needed. This can be carried out in a window. When lines of the hatch area outline become dotted in the **Break** window sequence, press Return twice and the next line in the sequence becomes dotted.

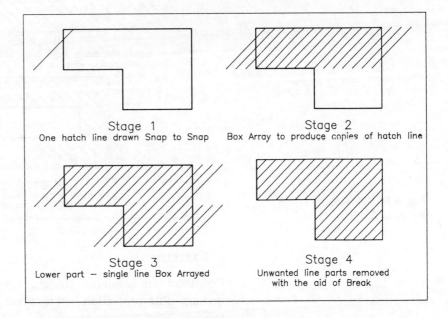

Fig. 9.12 Hatching with the aid of Box Array

Method 3: In Fig. 9.13, in which hatching does not extend across the circle, the hatch lines were broken away from the circles with the aid of **Break**.

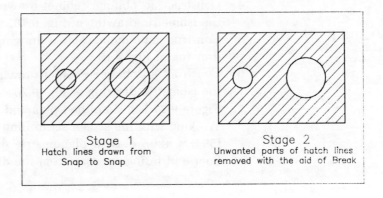

Fig. 9.13 Hatching with Snap and Break

The hatching of Fig. 9.14 was added to the drawing by first drawing a single hatch line across **Snap** points, then with **Box Array** copying the single line the required number of times. Unwanted parts of hatch lines were then removed with the aid of **Break**.

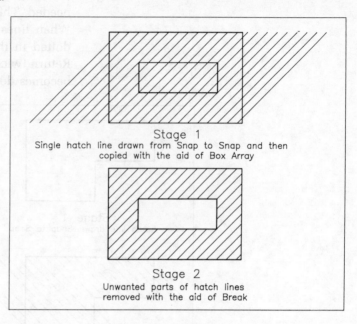

Stage 1
Single hatch line drawn from Snap to Snap and then copied with the aid of Box Array

Stage 2
Unwanted parts of hatch lines removed with the aid of Break

Fig. 9.14 Hatching with Box Array and Break

Exercises

1. Construct an isometric drawing of the part shown by the orthographic projection of Fig. 9.15.
2. Construct an isometric drawing of the item shown in the orthographic projection of Fig. 9.16.
3. Construct an isometric drawing of the bracket given in the orthographic drawing of Fig. 9.17.
4. Construct an oblique cabinet drawing of the slide shown by the isometric drawing of Fig. 9.18.
5. Construct an oblique cabinet drawing of the fork shown in the drawing of Fig. 9.19.
6. Construct an oblique cabinet drawing of the slide shown by the isometric drawing of Fig. 9.20.
7. Figure 9.21 is a simplified plan and front view of a bathroom. Working with the screen set to limits suitable for an A3 sheet (594 × 420), draw a planometric drawing of the two walls, floor and fittings as seen from the direction of the arrow.

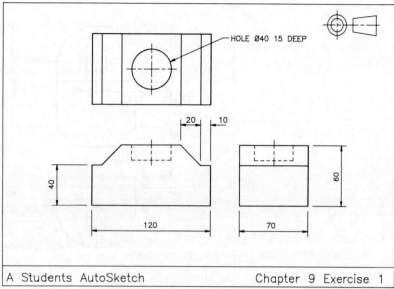

Fig. 9.15 Exercise 1

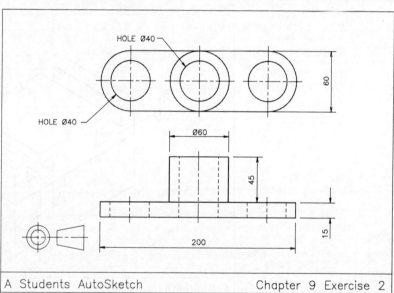

Fig. 9.16 Exercise 2

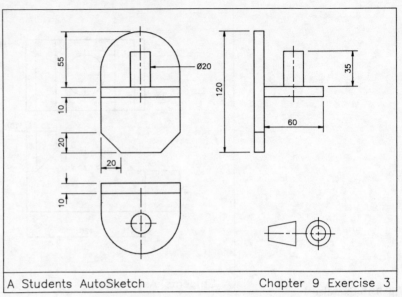

A Students AutoSketch   Chapter 9 Exercise 3

Fig. 9.17 Exercise 3

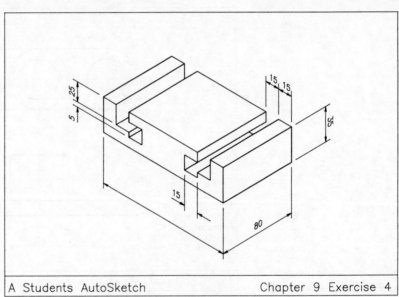

A Students AutoSketch   Chapter 9 Exercise 4

Fig. 9.18 Exercise 4

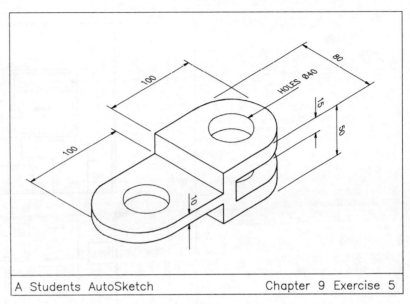

Fig. 9.19 Exercise 5

A Students AutoSketch   Chapter 9 Exercise 5

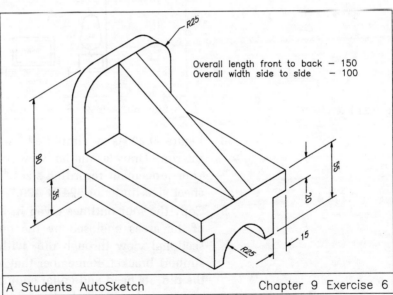

Fig. 9.20 Exercise 6

A Students AutoSketch   Chapter 9 Exercise 6

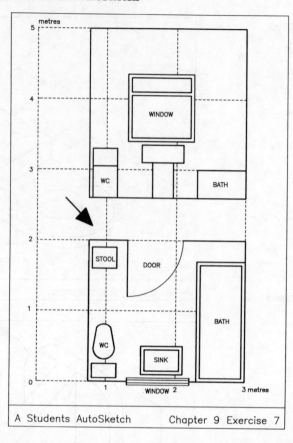

Fig. 9.21 Exercise 7

8. Figure 9.22 is a simplified isometric drawing of a room interior. Draw a similar view in planometric drawing. Use your judgement regarding sizes. Work on a screen set for A2 sheet size limits of 594 × 420.

9. Copy the four outlines given in Fig. 9.23. Section hatch each of the areas enclosed by the outlines. Drawing 3 shows a sectional view through pin, with head and collar held in a support bracket. Remember that when sectioning such items, the pin, its head and collar should be drawn as outside views and thus should not be hatched.

10. Figure 9.24 is a plan and sectional front view of a capped fitting. The drawing was drawn on an A3 sheet. The front view has not been section hatched. Copy the drawing, without including dimensions, and add all required section hatching. Remember that webs are not hatched, but shown as outside views in such sections.

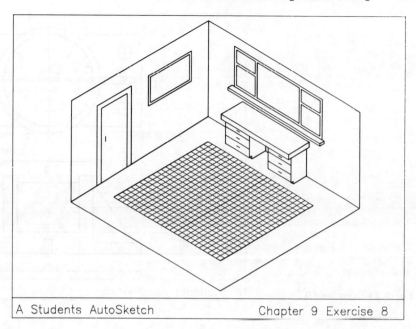

Fig. 9.22 Exercise 8

A Students AutoSketch   Chapter 9 Exercise 8

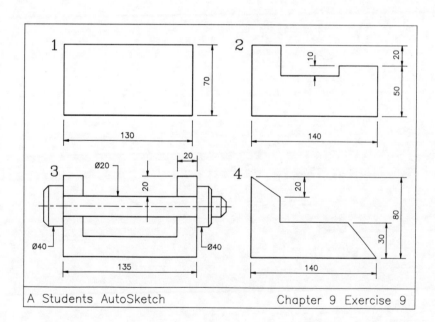

Fig. 9.23 Exercise 9

A Students AutoSketch   Chapter 9 Exercise 9

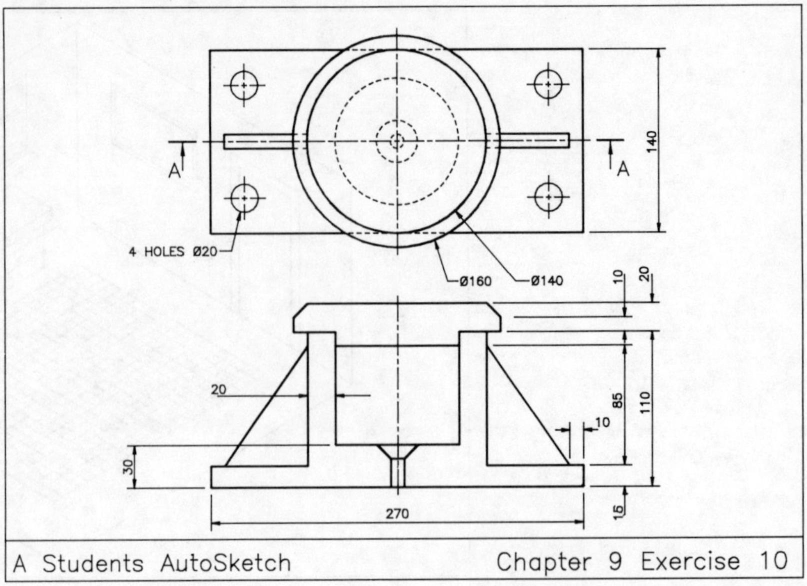

Fig. 9.24 Exercise 10

4 HOLES Ø20

Ø160 Ø140

140

10 20

20

85 110

30 10

270 16

A Students AutoSketch   Chapter 9 Exercise 10

CHAPTER 10

MS–DOS and Archimedes

MS–DOS

There are major differences in the manner of operation between an IBM PC computer working under MS–DOS and an Archimedes working under RISC OS. The actual operating systems need not concern us here. There are however some differences between the two command systems as they affect how AutoSketch is used.

Note: in either MS–DOS or in Archimedes, filenames can be typed in either capital or lower-case letters.

MS–DOS directories and sub-directories

In MS–DOS systems, files are saved in directories and sub-directories. As an example, a group of AutoSketch drawing files could be saved in a directory with the name of *draw*. In this directory, engineering drawings could be saved in a sub-directory with the name of *eng*. Also in the *draw* directory, building drawings could be saved in a sub-directory *build*. Other types of drawing could also be saved in sub-directories of the *draw* directory.

MS–DOS filenames

In MS–DOS systems, AutoSketch files are saved with a file name and a file extension. The filename can consist of any appropriate name with no more than eight letters. The filename extension is a full stop followed by three letters. The MS–DOS filename extension system of AutoSketch is as follows:

Drawing files are saved with an extension *.skd;*
Plot files are saved with an extension *.plt;*
Slide files are saved with an extension *.sld;*
DXF files are saved with an extension *.dxf;*

Backup files are saved with an extension *.bak*;
Font files have an extension *.shx*;

Note: each time the current drawing is saved, it is saved with a filename extension *.skd*. A backup file, with a filename extension *.bak* is automatically saved when the current AutoSketch drawing file is saved a second (or more) times.

As an example of files in the *draw* directory, in which there are three sub-directories *eng, build* and *elec*:

Directory		*draw*	
Sub-directories	*eng*	*build*	*elec*
Files	*bolt.skd*	*bricks.skd*	*lamps.skd*
	bolt.dxf	*bricks.dxf*	*lamps.dxf*
	bolt.plt	*bricks.plt*	*lamps.dxf*
	bolt.sld	*bricks.sld*	*lamps.sld*
	bolt.bak	*bricks.bak*	*lamps.bak*

In the directory *draw* the file *bolt.skd* will have a full filename of *draw\eng\bolt.skd*. In this full filename there is a back-slash between the directory, sub-directory and filename. The filename extension is separated from the filename by a full stop. The operator must decide on the name under which files are to be saved. When working within AutoSketch, the file name extension is omitted. In fact if a file name extension is keyed in at a dialogue box, the software does not respond.

Always take care with the actual naming of files. If AutoSketch is used extensively, a hard disc on a computer may contain hundreds of AutoSketch files. If each drawing file is not given a sensible name, the operator may have great difficulty in finding any one file from the large numbers that can be on a disc.

As an example of an AutoSketch filing system, the drawing, plot, slide and dxf files for the drawings in this book were saved in a directory *book*. The drawings for each chapter were saved in sub-directories *chap01, chap02* and so on. Each drawing had a filename such as *fig01*. From this the drawing Fig. 6.7 would have a full file name of:

$$book\chap06\fig07.skd$$

making that file quite distinct and easy to find from the many drawing files held on disc while this book was being written.

Incidentally, my directory *book* also contained sub-directories for plot and dxf files. These sub-directories were also in the chapter sub-directories. Thus the full name for the dxf file for my Fig. 6.7 is:

book\chap06\dxf\fig07.dxf

and the full plot filename for this drawing is:

book\chap06\plot\fig07.plt

Font files in MS–DOS

The fonts for AutoSketch text are held in files with the MS–DOS file extension *.shx*. AutoSketch font files are AutoCAD font files. This enables the swapping of drawings with text between AutoSketch and AutoCAD via DXF files to be carried out with ease. Remember however that not all details of AutoCAD files can be converted to AutoSketch files. However, the various fonts of AutoSketch will all convert to AutoCAD via DXF files.

MS–DOS commands

Several of the commands used with MS–DOS systems may be needed when working with AutoSketch.

Disc names in MS–DOS

In MS–DOS, the three main disc types are named by letters:
Floppy discs   a: b:
Hard disc   c:

Cataloguing disc contents in MS–DOS

To show on screen the contents of any directory in MS–DOS, at the disc drive prompt, type *dir* followed by the directory name:

A:\\>dir book\chap06   *Keyboard   Return*

and a list of files held in that directory will appear on screen. The following is an example:

C:\\>dir sketch   *Keyboard   Return*

.		<DIR>	2-11-89	
..		<DIR>	2-11-89	
SKETCH	OVL	270272	12-10-09	4:00p
SKETCH	EXE	112688	12-10-89	4:00p
FLOPPY	BAT	233	12-10-89	4:00p
DS8514	EXE	43920	12-10-89	4:00p
DSMCGA	EXE	18144	12-10-89	4:00p

ROMANS	SHX	4926	12-10-89	4:00p
ROMANC	SHX	6901	12-10-89	4:00p
SCRIPTC	SHX	7699	12-10-89	4:00p
ITALICC	SHX	7483	12-10-89	4:00p
SYMAP	SHX	6103	12-10-89	4:00p
SYMATH	SHX	6035	12-10-89	4:00p
SYMUSIC	SHX	6910	12-10-89	4:00p
MONOTXT	SHX	2828	12-10-89	4:00p
SKETCH3	MID	173	12-10-89	4:00p
SKETCH	CFG	235	19-09-90	10:53a
DRAW	<DIR>		14-12-89	3:45p

20 files   6680576 bytes free

C:\>

Making directories in MS–DOS

At the disc prompt:

A:\>mkdir draw\part *Keyboard   Return*

and the sub-directory *part* would be made on the disc in directory *draw* on the disc in drive A. If in the hard disc drive C:

C:\> mkdir a:\draw\part   *Keyboard   Return*

forms the sub-directory *part* in the directory *draw* on the disc in drive A.

Note: the abbreviation **md** can be used instead of **mkdir.**

Erasing files from discs in MS–DOS

At the disc prompt:

C:\>erase a:\draw\part\nut.skd   *Keyboard   Return*

removes the named file from disc in drive A.

One example of file erasure which you may have to carry out is when you wish to re-configure AutoSketch. The first step in this process is to erase the file *sketch.cfg* from the directory in which the AutoSketch software files are held:

C:\>erase sketch\sketch.cfg   *Keyboard   Return*

When AutoSketch is then re-loaded into the computer a series of prompts appears to re-configure the digitiser, the monitor type and the plotter and the port to which it is attached. When the prompts for these configuration details have been answered a new *sketch.cfg* file is automatically made within the directory *sketch*.

Archimedes

Archimedes directories and sub-directories

Directories and sub-directories are used for storing files in the Archimedes systems in a similar manner to MS–DOS systems. However file name extensions are not used in Archimedes. This means that drawing, plot, dxf, slide and bak files must be held in their own sub-directories. Note that in Archimedes a * must precede any command. Fail to include the * and the command does not become effective. Taking again examples from a *draw* directory, in Archimedes, the directory and sub-directory set up will be:

Directory		*draw*	
Sub-directories	*eng*	*build*	*elec*
Sub-directory	*skd*	*skd*	*skd*
Files	*bolt*	*bricks*	*lamps*
Sub-directory	*dxf*	*dxf*	*dxf*
Files	*bolt*	*bricks*	*lamps*
Sub-directory	*plt*	*plt*	*plt*
Files	*bolt*	*bricks*	*lamps*
Sub-directory	*sld*	*sld*	*sld*
Files	*bolt*	*bricks*	*lamps*
Sub-directory	*bak*	*bak*	*bak*
Files	*bolt*	*bricks*	*lamps*

In Archimedes, back-slashes are replaced by fullstops. Thus the full file name of the bolt drawing in Archimedes will be:

draw.eng.skd.bolt

In Archimedes AutoSketch, my Fig. 6.7 drawing would have the file name:

book.chap06.skd.fig07

Of particular importance in Archimedes is the fact that the sub-directories *skd*, *plt*, etc., MUST be on the disc before drawing or plot files can be saved. If these sub-directories do not exist, it may not be possible to save the file. If the sub-directories do not exist on the disc, a warning dialogue box may appear stating that the sub-directory will be automatically formed, enabling the drawing, plot or other type of file to be saved.

Font files in Archimedes

Font files in Archimedes are held in the sub-directory *shx*.

Archimedes commands

In Archimedes the three main disc types are named by figures:

Floppy discs   :0   :1
Hard disc   :4

The screen prompt is: >-   i.e., the disc drive number does not appear at the prompt.

Cataloguing discs in Archimedes

In Archimedes at the disc drive prompt type either:

>*cat *Keyboard   Return*

or just:

>*. *Keyboard   Return*

and a list of files held on the disc in the current drive appears on screen.

If the current drive is different from that being catalogued:

>*cat :0 *Keyboard   Return*

will result in the names of files held in the named disc appearing on screen.

To catalogue the contents of a directory:

>*.:0.SKETCH *Keyboard   Return*
SKETCH Disc HARDISK :4 Option 00(Off) URD "Unset"

BAK   D   DXF D   PLT D   SKD D   SLD D
SPRITE D
>

In this example note the following:

1. Each sub-directory is shown as being such by the letter D (directory) appearing after its name.
2. In Archimedes, *sprites* can be drawn in AutoSketch. Archimedes sprites are graphic images which will load into other software programmes. When not in AutoSketch, sprites can be included in some brands of Archimedes word-processing and

Desktop editing software. This facility is not available in MS–DOS systems because it is peculiar to Archimedes.

Making directories in Archimedes

>*CDIR :0.DRAW.PARTS *Keyboard Return*

will form the sub-directory *parts* in the directory *draw* on the disc in drive :0.

Erasing files in Archimedes

>*delete :0.draw.parts.nut *Keyboard Return*
will erase the file *draw.parts.nut* from the disc in drive :0.
The AutoSketch configuration file is named *SKETCHCFG* and is held in the directory *RESOURCES*. If you wish to re-configure AutoSketch, to erase the configuration file:
>*DELETE :4.RESOURCES.SKETCHCFG *Keyboard Return*
deletes the file and allows the software to be re-configured.

CHAPTER 11

Revision Exercises

Introduction

This chapter contains a number of exercises which can be drawn using CAD software. They are included here as a revision of the various methods of constructing drawings in CAD as they have been described in this book. The exercises are of increasing difficulty and readers may find that to attempt the last four or five requires a considerable level of skill and experience. Hints on how to proceed with the exercises are included with each exercise.

Exercises

1. Draw a three-view orthographic projection of the block shown by the isometric drawing Fig. 11.1. Work in First Angle.
   (a) work on a screen with **Limits** set to 420,297 (A3);
   (b) set **Grid** to 10 and **Snap** to 5;
   (c) use **Snap** or relative coordinates to construct the parts of the drawing to their correct unit sizes;
   (d) construct three rectangles of overall sizes for each of the three views on a construction layer. This layer can be turned off when the drawing is completed;
   (e) include hidden detail in all views;
   (f) fully dimension the drawing using the **Part** method of dimensioning outlined on page 77;
   (g) add a suitable title block with your name, the scale (1:1) and a name for the block.
2. Draw a three-view orthographic projection of the block shown by the isometric drawing Fig. 11.2. Work in Third Angle;
   (a) set the screen to **Limits** of 420,297 (A3);
   (b) set **Grid** to 10 and snap set to 5 to draw to correct unit sizes with 1 coordinate unit = 1 mm;
   (c) or use the relative coordinates method of ensuring the parts of the drawing are of correct unit sizes;

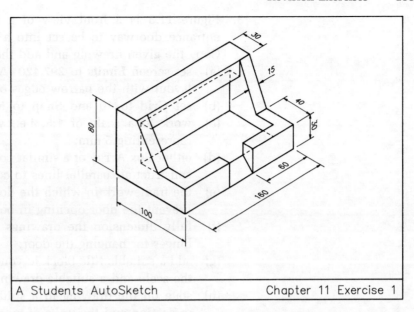

Fig. 11.1 Exercise 1 | A Students AutoSketch | Chapter 11 Exercise 1

(d) construct three rectangles of overall sizes for each of the three views on a construction layer. This layer can be turned off when the drawing is completed;

(e) add hidden detail to all views;

(f) fully dimension the completed views – use the **Part** method of dimensioning outlined on page 77;

(g) add a suitable title block with your name, the scale (1:1) and a name for the block.

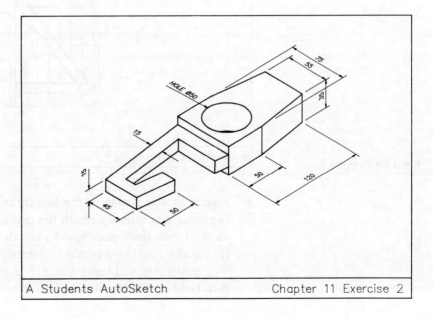

Fig. 11.2 Exercise 2 | A Students AutoSketch | Chapter 11 Exercise 2

3. Figure 11.3 is a front view of a braced door for a garden entrance doorway to be set into a 115 mm thick brick wall. Copy the given drawing and add the sectional view on A–A;

   (a) set screen **Limits** to 297,420 (A3). Note this is in portrait layout with the narrow edges of the sheet horizontal;

   (b) set **Grid** to 10 and **Snap** to 5;

   (c) work to a scale of 1:5, i.e., with each coordinate unit representing 5 mm;

   (d) either **Box Array** or a similar command will be required to construct all parallel lines to correct unit sizes;

   (e) the framework in which the door is set requires a stop to prevent the door opening in both directions;

   (f) fully dimension the drawings and add a suitable set of hinges for hanging the door;

   (g) add a suitable title block to your drawing with your name, the scale and a suitable drawing title;

   (h) state on the drawing in a suitable position, the angle of projection and the units of measurements used.

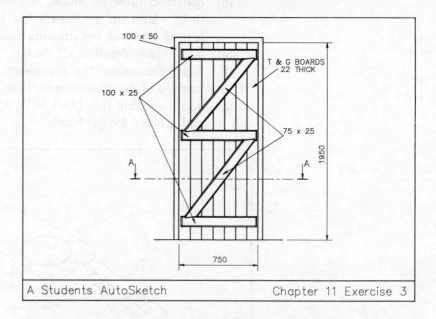

Fig. 11.3 Exercise 3

4. Figure 11.4 is a plan of the handle from a selection device. As the handle is turned so both the cylindrical pins and the square slots fit into their positions in the device;

   (a) make a full size (scale 1:1) drawing of the handle within a screen set to **Limits** 420,297 (A3);

   (b) **Grid** and **Snap** should be set to 10 and 5 respectively;

(c) there are twelve repeats of the finger curves, the plans of the pins and the square slots. Only draw one set before applying the command **Ring Array** (or similar);

(d) add centre-lines and dimensions after completing the array;

(e) add a suitable title block to the drawing.

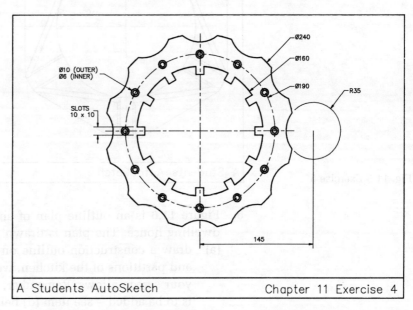

Fig. 11.4 Exercise 4

5. Figure 11.5 is another **Ring Array** (or similar command system) exercise. Some judgement or adjustment is required to ensure that the 8 mm wide webs are correctly positioned in the array;

(a) work on a screen set to **Limits** of 420,297 (A3);

(b) set **Grid** to 10 and **Snap** to 5. Work to full size (scale 1:1);

(c) start by drawing one of the bosses (those parts of 28 mm width) and **Ring Array** it six times around the central point;

(d) draw either the left- or right-hand side of the two webs (those parts which are 8 mm wide) and array it three times around the central point. Then draw the other web and array that three times;

(e) some use of **Break** and **Erase** will be found to be necessary;

(f) the hexagonal edges and the central circle can be drawn with **Line** after the array is complete. Some erasure of arcs at the base of each boss will need to be deleted with **Break**.

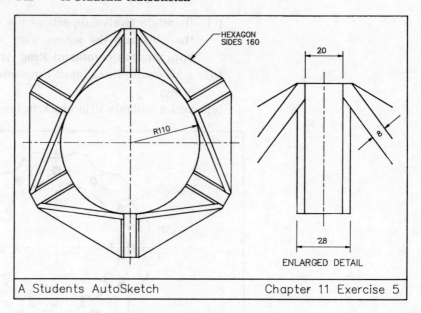

HEXAGON SIDES 160

20

R110

8

28

ENLARGED DETAIL

A Students AutoSketch   Chapter 11 Exercise 5

Fig. 11.5 Exercise 5

6. Figure 11.6 is an outline plan of an empty kitchen in a small dwelling house. The plan is drawn on a grid of 1 m squares;
    (a) draw a construction outline on its own layer of the walls and partitions of the kitchen, working to as large a scale as your screen allows. Remember, however, that a front view is to be added – see item (d) below. The construction layer can be turned off when the drawing is completed;
    (b) copy the details in the given drawing. The wall and partition thicknesses can be accurately drawn with the aid of **Box Array** (or similar). Either insert the doors with the aid of the **Part** command, or draw one and then copy it to the other positions;
    (c) add the following items in the plan: a double-sink unit; suitable storage cupboards and drawers; a refrigerator; a cooker; a washing machine; dishwasher;
    (d) add a front view as seen looking from the direction of the wall which contains the serving hatch;
    (e) fully dimension the drawing and add a suitable title block.
7. A three-view First Angle orthographic projection of a head from a drilling machine is given in Fig. 11.7. Sizes not given are left to your own judgement;
    (a) work on a screen set to **Limits** of 594,420 (A2) with **Grid** set to 10 and **Snap** set to 5;
    (b) draw an overall construction layout for three views in Third Angle projection on a separate layer which can be

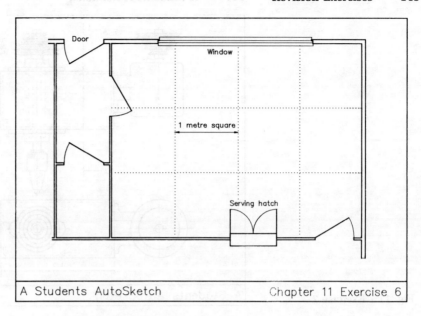

Fig. 11.6 Exercise 6

turned off when the drawing is completed;

(c) the spindle on which the pulley and chuck are fixed runs inside a sleeve to ensure smooth running of the spindle when the drill is in action;

(d) draw the following three view:
   (i) the given front view in section;
   (ii) the given end view as an outside view;
   (iii) the given plan;

(e) do not dimension the drawing but add a suitable title block and statements of dimensioning units and angle of projection.

8. Copy the sectional drawing through part of the roof of a bungalow given by Fig. 11.8. Work to any suitable scale. Polar ordinates will be required to obtain the 30° roof slope and **Box Array** (or a similar command) will be needed to draw the parallel lines. Add all the lettering. Add a suitable title block.

9. Figure 11.9 is a half section through the front of a building. No dimensions are included with this drawing. Work to sizes of your own choice on a screen set to **Limits** 594,420 (A2). In order to construct such a drawing, frequent use of **Zoom** will be required;

(a) draw construction outlines for the front lines and floor lines on a separate layer, which can be turned off when the drawing is completed;

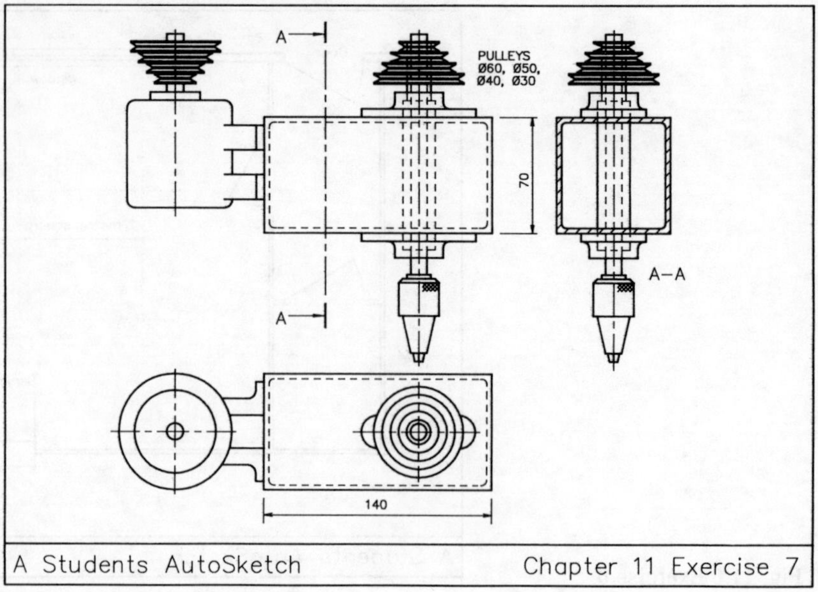

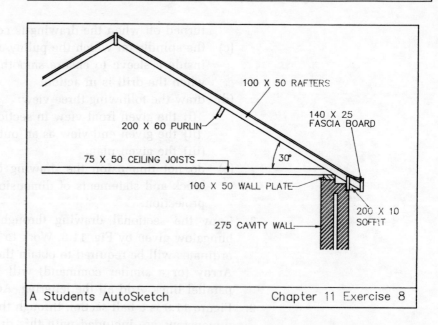

Fig. 11.7 Exercise 7

A Students AutoSketch   Chapter 11 Exercise 7

Fig. 11.8 Exercise 8

A Students AutoSketch   Chapter 11 Exercise 8

(b) draw, as accurately as possible, the various features shown in the Fig. 11.9;

(c) **Box Array** will be required to draw the many parallel lines;

(d) add suitable lettering describing the various features of the drawing;

(e) add a suitable title block which includes a title for the

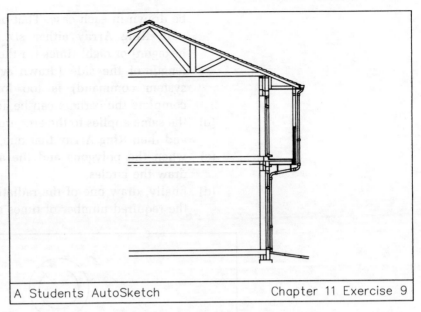

Fig. 11.9 Exercise 9

A Students AutoSketch   Chapter 11 Exercise 9

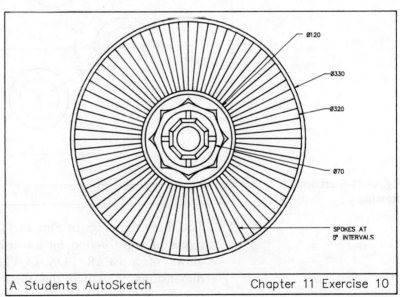

Fig. 11.10 Exercise 10

A Students AutoSketch   Chapter 11 Exercise 10

drawing, your name and the scale to which the drawing was made.

10. Figure 11.10 is a front view of an electric fan. The fan is covered by a protective wire guard. Copy the given drawing on a screen set to **Limits** 594,420 (A2) to the dimensions given. This is an exercise in the use of **Ring Array** (or similar command). Note the following:

(a) to draw both the hexagon and octagon, only one side need be drawn in each case. That one side can then be arrayed with **Ring Array** either six times (in the case of the hexagon) or eight times (in the case of the octagon). If the length of the side (drawn with the relative coordinate system command) is too long, when the polygon is complete the corners can be adjusted with **Break**;

(b)   the same applies to the arcs around the hexagon. Draw one and then **Ring Array** that one;

(c)   when the polygons and the arcs have been drawn then draw the circles;

(d)   finally, draw one of the radiating lines and **Ring Array** it the required number of times around the circles.

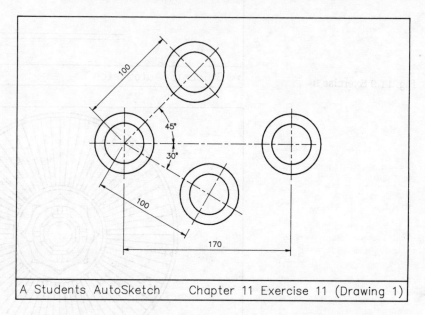

Fig. 11.11 Exercise 11 – drawing 1

A Students AutoSketch   Chapter 11 Exercise 11 (Drawing 1)

11.   The three drawings of Figs 11.11, 11.12 and 11.13 show the stages of construction for an orthographic projection in two views of a GEAR BOX COVER. Figure 11.11 gives the dimensions to which the three groups of two concentric circles are to be drawn, Fig. 11.12 is the completed plan, Fig. 11.13 shows a sectional view on A–A of Fig. 11.12.

(a)   Work on a screen set to **Limits** of 594,420 (A2) with **Grid** set to 10 and **Snap** set to 5;

(b)   draw a construction grid for the centre lines of the pairs of circles on a separate layer which can be turned off when the drawing is complete;

(c)   draw the three pairs of circles;

(d)   from the same centres construct the remainder of the plan;

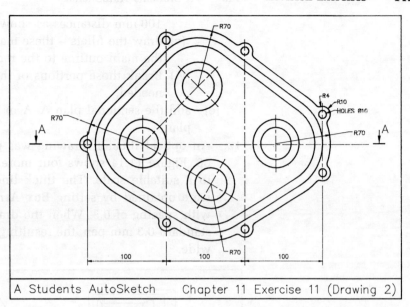

**Fig. 11.12 Exercise 11 –
drawing 2**

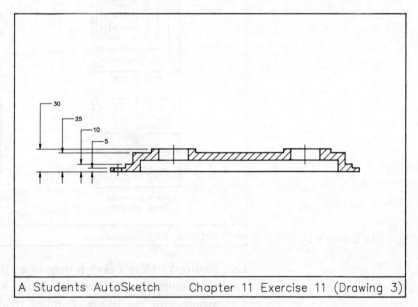

**Fig. 11.13 Exercise 11 –
drawing 3**

(i) draw circles of radii 50, 60 and 70 from the centres of the circles drawn in (c) above;

(ii) make sure that **Attach** is on to ensure that lines can be drawn which touch and so are tangential to these circles;

(iii) draw the lines tangential to the circles and **Break** those portions of the circles not needed;

(iv) draw circles of diameter 10 and radius 10 at the

100 mm distances as shown;

    (v) draw the fillets – these may have to be arcs – joining the main outline to the radius 10 circles;

    (vi) **Break** those portions of the radius 10 arcs no longer needed;

(e) add the sectional plan A–A in correct projection with the plan.

12. An optical illusion drawing was given in Fig. 5.16 on page 68. Figure 11.14 shows four more. Draw these four illusions to a suitable scale. The thick lines of two of the drawings were obtained by setting **Box Array** to 3 rows, or columns with spacing of 0.3. When the drawings were plotted with a standard 0.3 mm pen, the resulting lines were plotted 0.9 mm wide.

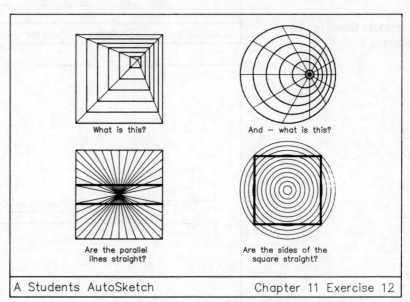

Fig. 11.14 Exercise 12

13. Figure 11.15 is a sketch map of a village drawn with the aid of CAD software. Construct a similar sketch map of an area near where you are living. Parallel road widths can be obtained with the aid of **Box Array**, arcs at road joins can be drawn with the aid of **Fillet**.

14. An underside view of Concorde in flight is shown in Fig. 11.16. Draw a similar view of any other plane of your choice. The curved lines were drawn with the aid of **Curve** with **Frame** on to allow for adjustments. Only half of the view was constructed, the other half being copied with the **Mirror** command system.

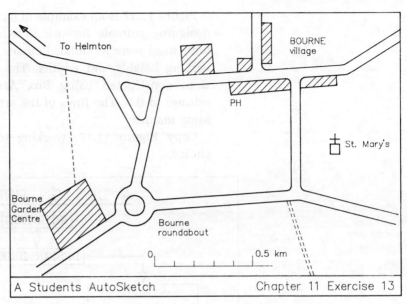

Fig. 11.15 Exercise 13

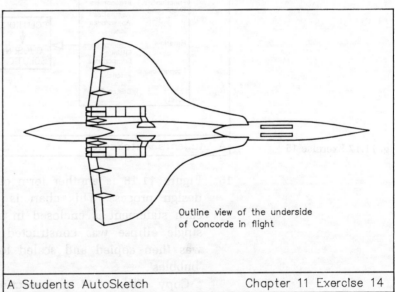

Fig. 11.16 Exercise 14

15. Block diagrams, charts of various types, posters, notices of forthcoming events and similar graphics involving text, can all be drawn with the aid of the **Text** command system. AutoSketch includes four font files (files ending in the extension .shx). Each font can be drawn on screen at any height, width, slope and oblique angle by selecting **Settings** and keying the necessary sizes at appropriate places in the **Text** dialogue box.

Figure 11.17 is an example of a chart describing a method of designing suitable for use in educational institutions. The fonts used were Monotxt, Romans, Romanc and Italicc, set to varying heights and widths. The thicker lines of the boxes were constructed using **Box Array** with column or row settings of 0.3. The lines of the arrows were thickened in the same manner.

Copy Figure 11.17, working to font sizes of your own choice.

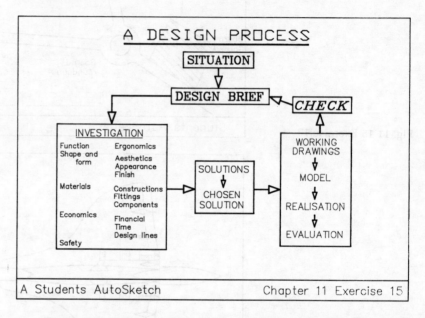

Fig. 11.17 Exercise 15

16. Figure 11.18 is another form of chart describing a similar design process. This chart is a 'bubble' chart in which each statement is enclosed in an ellipse or in a circle. A single ellipse was constructed from arcs of circles. This was then copied and scaled to give the varying sizes of 'bubbles'.

Copy Figure 11.18, selecting fonts to give text of varying heights, widths and slopes.

Work disc

A work disc containing files of starter drawings with instructions for all the exercises in this book can be obtained as follows:

Cost: £6.00 each disc. Cheques or Postal Orders payable to A. Yarwood.

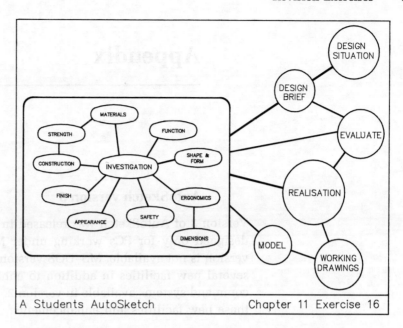

A Students AutoSketch   Chapter 11 Exercise 16

Fig. 11.18 Exercise 16

Archimedes – 3½ inch (1 disc) or 5¼ inch (1 disc);
MS–DOS IBM PC compatible – 5¼ inch – 360 K (2 discs), or 1.2 K (1 disc); – 3½ inch – 720 K (1 disc)

When ordering state type of computer and disc format required.

From: 10 Tinneys Close,
         Woodfalls,
         Salisbury SP5 2LU

Allow 15 working days for delivery.

The exercises on the disc form a comprehensive course of work for those interested in gaining CAD drawing skills.

Note: it is necessary to have a copy of the book if you wish to use the work disc. The work disc contains AutoSketch starter drawing files for the exercise together with instructions for completing them. The exercise drawings and texts on which these starter drawings are based are not included.

Appendix

AutoSketch version 3

Version 3 of AutoSketch was released in 1991. This new release is designed only for PCs working under MS–DOS. An Archimedes version is not available. MS–DOS version 3 of AutoSketch includes several new facilities in addition to enhancements to some of the command systems available in version 2. This Appendix deals with these new facilities and enhancements.

Screen editor

When AutoSketch version 3 is loaded the very first time, one of the configuration tasks is to decide whether scrollbars for panning are required. This is a new facility. In this book practically all the exercises are based on working within a screen configured for A3 sheet drawings. Because of this, it is advisable at this stage to reply N (No) to whether scrollbars are required or not. Figure A1 shows the version 3 scrollbars. At a later date the no scrollbars decision can be reversed by deleting the file *sketch.cfg* and re-configuring the software by answering Y (Yes) to the scrollbars request. Note that this configuration is only performed the very first time AutoSketch version 3 is loaded into the computer.

Function keys

In version 2 many of the commands could be called by pressing either one of the function keys (those labelled F1 to F10 on the keyboard) or by pressing both the Alt key and one of the function keys. In version 3 a further ten commands can be called by pressing the Ctrl key and one of the function keys. These new Ctrl+F key calls are shown in Fig. A2. An adhesive strip with these new key calls printed on its surface is provided with newly purchased

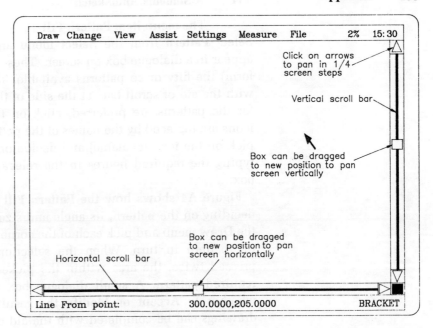

Draw Change View Assist Settings Measure File 2% 15:30

Click on arrows
to pan in 1/4
screen steps

Vertical scroll bar

Box can be dragged
to new position to pan
screen vertically

Box can be dragged
to new position to pan
screen horizontally

Horizontal scroll bar

Line From point: 300.0000,205.0000 BRACKET

Fig. A1 The AutoSketch
version 3 screen with
scrollbars

software. This enhancement allows an increase in the speed of working with the software.

Fig. A2 A suggested strip to show Function key commands

Amendments to the Draw menu

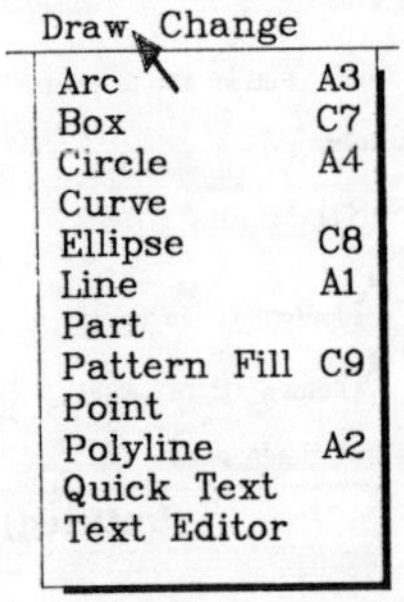

The version 3 Draw menu is shown in Fig. A3. New facilities included are: **Ellipse**; **Pattern Fill**; **Polyline**; **Quick Text** and **Text Editor**.

The menu item Ellipse

Select **Ellipse** from the **Settings** menu. It will be seen that three options are offered for the way in which an ellipse can be drawn:

Center and Both Axes;

Axis and Planar Rotation;

Two Foci and Point.

Fig. A3 The version 3 Draw
pull-down menu

To draw an ellipse, choose the method desired from the **Settings** menu, select **Ellipse** from the **Draw** menu and follow the instructions given by the prompts appearing at the prompt line of the screen.

The menu item Pattern Fill

Select **Pattern** from the **Select** menu and a series of icons will appear in a dialogue box on screen. These icons show (in miniature form) the fifty or so patterns available. The icons can be scrolled with the aid of scroll bars at the side of the dialogue box. If names for the patterns are preferred, click on the word **Names** and the icons are replaced by the names of the patterns. To choose a pattern pick on the icon (or name) and decide on the **Angle** and **Scale** by typing the required figures in the relevant boxes of the dialogue box.

Figure A4 shows how the **Pattern Fill** command is used. After deciding on the pattern, its angle and size, select **Pattern Fill** from the **Draw** menu and pick each of the corners of the required area for the pattern in turn. When the selection device pick button is pressed twice, the area within the picked area is filled with the required pattern. A small dialogue box then appears requesting whether to **Accept** or **Modify** the result. Hatching of sectional drawings can be completed with the aid of a selected **Pattern** and the menu item **Pattern Fill**.

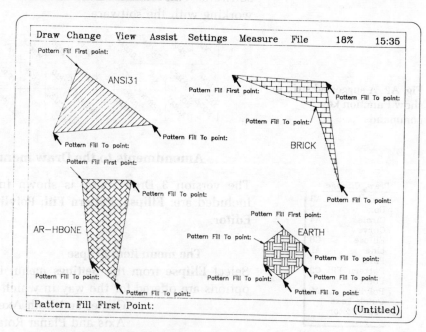

Fig. A4 Examples of Pattern Fill

The menu item Polyline

Polyline replaces the version 2 menu item **Polygon**. **Polyline** however has the advantage over **Polygon** that width, whether it is to be filled, blank or patterned, can be adjusted. To draw a **Polyline** first select **Polyline** from the **Select** menu. The dialogue box (Fig.

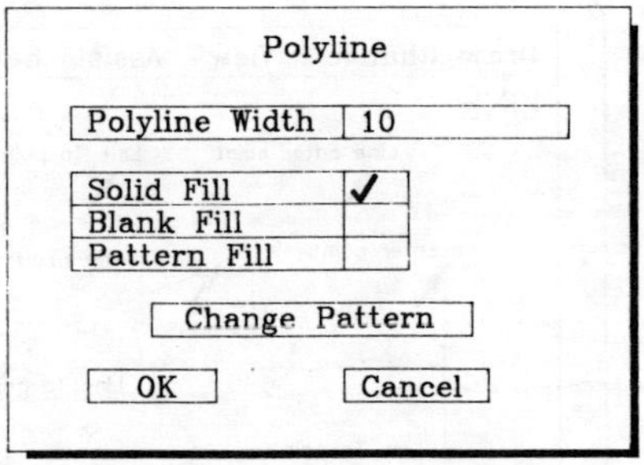

Fig. A5 The Polyline
dialogue box

A5) appears on the screen. Enter the required **Polyline** width and whether it is to be solid, blank or patterned. If patterned, the required pattern must also be selected from the **Pattern** dialogue box. Then draw the **Polyline** as required. Figure A6 shows a number of polylines. Note that they can be acted upon by **Fillet** or **Chamfer**. **Polyline** arcs can only be drawn if **Arc Mode** (**Assist** menu) is on.

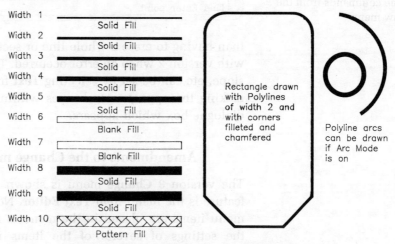

Fig. A6 Examples of version
3 polylines

Figure A7 shows (in the bottom right corner) the prompts associated with Polyline.

The menu item Quick Text
This functions in the same manner as **Text** from version 2.

The menu item Text Editor
The **Text Editor** allows text to be amended before it is inserted into a drawing. If a fair quantity of text is to be inserted in a drawing, use the **Text Editor**. This allows spelling mistakes or incorrect wording to be changed before being placed in a drawing, rather

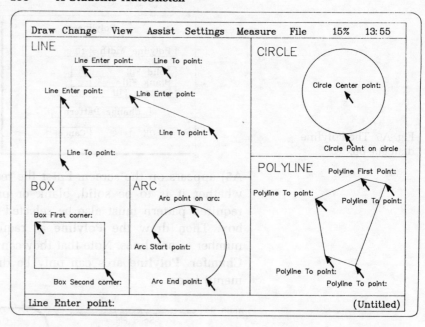

Fig. A7 Methods of using some commands from the Draw menu

than having to erase a whole line or section of text as was the case with version 2 when an error occurred. The text font, height, width, slope, etc can be set by selecting **Text** from the **Settings** menu and making the appropriate changes within the **Text and Font Mode** dialogue box which appears.

Amendments to the Change menu

The version 3 **Change** menu is shown in Fig. A8. The only new feature is the menu item **Text Editor**. Note that the order in which menu items are placed in the menu is now alphabetical. Because the settings of several of the items in the Change menu are controlled under items in the **Settings** menu, it is included in Fig. A8.

The menu item Text Editor

The same dialogue box is used as that when this item is chosen from the **Draw** menu. The difference is that it only appears after picking the text on screen which is to be edited.

Amendments to the Assist menu

Figure A9 shows the **Assist** menu. Several new menu items are included in the version 3 Assist menu – **Arc Mode**; **View Icons**;

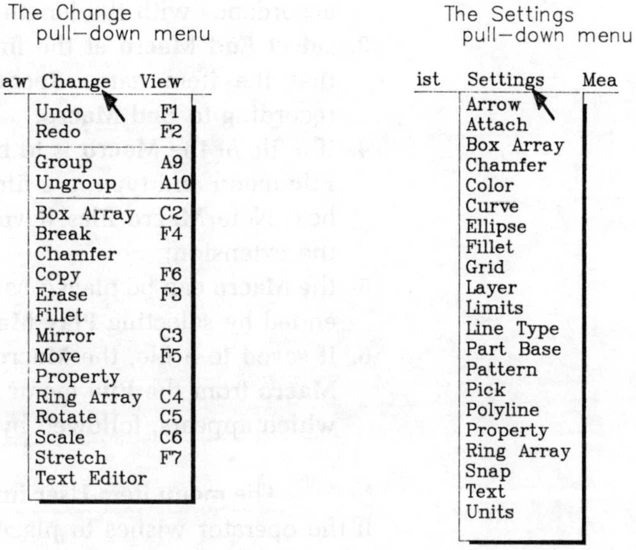

The Change
pull–down menu

aw	Change	View
	Undo	F1
	Redo	F2
	Group	A9
	Ungroup	A10
	Box Array	C2
	Break	F4
	Chamfer	
	Copy	F6
	Erase	F3
	Fillet	
	Mirror	C3
	Move	F5
	Property	
	Ring Array	C4
	Rotate	C5
	Scale	C6
	Stretch	F7
	Text Editor	

The Settings
pull–down menu

ist	Settings	Mea
	Arrow	
	Attach	
	Box Array	
	Chamfer	
	Color	
	Curve	
	Ellipse	
	Fillet	
	Grid	
	Layer	
	Limits	
	Line Type	
	Part Base	
	Pattern	
	Pick	
	Polyline	
	Property	
	Ring Array	
	Snap	
	Text	
	Units	

Fig. A8 The version 3
Change and Settings
pull-down menus

ew	Assist	Settings
	Arc Mode	C1
	Attach	A8
	Coord	
	Fill	
	Frame	
	✓Grid	A6
	Ortho	A5
	✓Snap	A7
	✓View Icons	
	Record Macro	
	Play Macro	
	User Input	C10

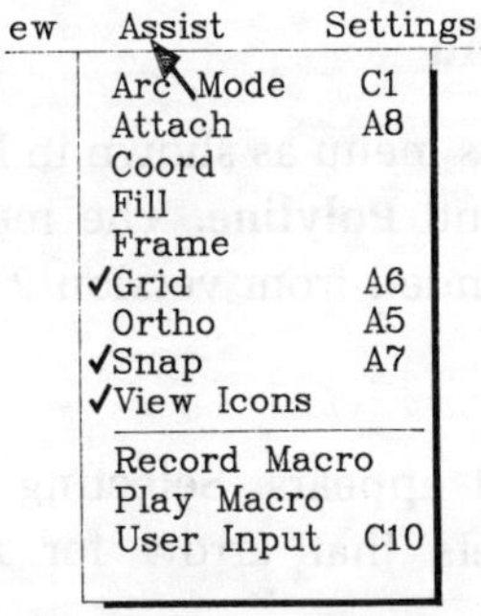

Fig. A9 The version 3 Assist
pull-down menu

Record Macro; **Play Macro**; **User Input**. All items other than the **Macro** and **User Input** items in the **Assist** are switched on or off by selecting the item when the **Assist** pull-down menu is showing. If on a tick will be seen against the item. If off there will be no tick.

The menu item Arc Mode
When on, this menu item allows arcs to be drawn in polylines.

The menu item View Icons
Several of the dialogue boxes in version 3 show details in icon form – e.g. drawing files are shown in miniature form. Examples are the **Pattern Setting** and the **Select Drawing File** dialogue boxes. If the menu item **View Icons** is off, names appear in place of icons within these dialogue boxes.

The menu items Record Macro and Play Macro
A **Macro** in AutoSketch is a file containing details of a series of AutoSketch operations. When a **Macro** is played (**Play Macro**) the series of operations is played back on the screen. An example would be a **Macro** played back during a lecture illustrated by AutoSketch drawings. The sequence of operations to construct a drawing in AutoSketch can also be recorded as a **Macro**.
The sequence of operations is:
1. select **Record Macro** from the **Assist** menu;
2. perform all the operations to be recorded in the macro – e.g. opening a series of files, timing their appearance on screen in

accordance with the length of time they are to be displayed;

3. select **End Macro** at the finish of the required recording. Note that the item name **Record Macro** has changed during the recording to **End Macro**;

4. if a file of the **Macro** is to be kept, select **Make Macro** from the **File** menu and type in a filename when promoted in a dialogue box. Note **Macro** files have an extension .*mcr*. Do not include the extension;

5. the **Macro** can be played back just after it has been recorded and ended by selecting **Play Macro** from the **Assist** menu;

6. if saved to a file, the **Macro** can be replayed by selecting **Read Macro** from the **File** menu and selecting from the dialogue box which appears, followed by **Play Macro** from the **Assist** menu.

The menu item User input

If the operator wishes to place a detail in the middle of a **Macro**, select this menu item and, e.g., type a text title on screen to appear in the **Macro** recording.

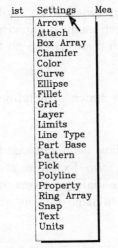

Fig. A10 The version 3
Settings menu

Amendments to the Settings menu

Four new version 3 items can be seen in this menu as shown in Fig. A10. These are **Arrow; Ellipse; Pattern** and **Polyline**. The menu items **Property** and **Attach** have been amended from version 2.

The menu item Arrow

When selected, the dialogue box Fig. A11 appears. Selecting the box against the required arrow type sets that arrow for any subsequent dimensioning.

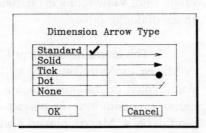

Fig. A11 The version 3
Dimension Arrow Type
dialogue box

The menu items **Ellipse, Pattern** and **Polyline**. See under the **Draw** menu above (page 153).

The menu item Attach

The attachment points possible when **Attach** (**Assist** menu) is on

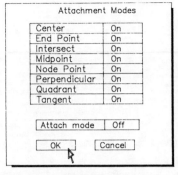

Fig. A12 The version 3
Attachment Modes dialogue
box

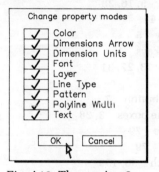

Fig. A13 The version 3
Change Property Modes
dialogue box

Fig. A14 The version 3 File
pull-down menu

have been increased in number. Figure A12 shows the new version
3 **Attachment Modes** dialogue box.

The menu item Property

The **Property** dialogue box also contains a number of new
elements. These are shown in Fig. A13.

Amendments to the File menu

Three new menu items are now included in this menu – **Part Clip**,
Make Macro and **Read Macro**. **Make Macro** and **Read Macro** have
already been dealt with (page 157). The version 3 File menu is
shown in Fig. A14.

The menu item Part Clip

Selecting this menu item allows part of a drawing to be selected as
a drawing for a part file. See Chapter 6.

Index